STAN STEINDL

THE GIFTS OF COMPASSION

How to understand and overcome suffering

AUSTRALIANACADEMIC**PRESS**

Other books in this series:
The Gifts of Compassion Personal Practice Workbook

First published 2020 by:
Australian Academic Press Group Pty. Ltd.
Samford Valley QLD, Australia
www.australianacademicpress.com.au

Copyright © 2020 Stan Steindl.

Copying for educational purposes
The *Australian Copyright Act 1968* (Cwlth) allows a maximum of one chapter or 10% of this book, whichever is the greater, to be reproduced and/or communicated by any educational institution for its educational purposes provided that the educational institution (or the body that administers it) has given a remuneration notice to Copyright Agency Limited (CAL) under the Act.
For details of the CAL licence for educational institutions contact:
Copyright Agency Limited, 19/157 Liverpool Street, Sydney, NSW 2000.
E-mail info@copyright.com.au

Production and communication for other purposes
Except as permitted under the Act, for example a fair dealing for the purposes of study, research, criticism or review, no part of this book may be reproduced, stored in a retrieval system, or transmitted in any form or by any means electronic, mechanical, photocopying, recording or otherwise without prior written permission of the copyright holder.

A catalogue record for this book is available from the National Library of Australia

The Gifts of Compassion: How to understand and overcome suffering
ISBN 9781925644487   (paperback)
ISBN 9781925644494   (ebook)

Disclaimer
Every effort has been made in preparing this work to provide information based on accepted standards and practice at the time of publication. The publisher and author, however, make no representations or warranties with respect to the accuracy or completeness of the contents of this book and specifically disclaim any implied warranties of merchantability or fitness for a particular purpose. It is sold on the understanding that the publisher is not engaged in rendering professional services and neither the publisher nor the author shall be liable for damages arising herefrom. If professional advice or other expert assistance is required, the services of a competent professional should be sought.

Publisher & Editor: Stephen May
Cover design: Luke Harris, Working Type Studio
Typesetting: Australian Academic Press
Printing: Lightning Source

To my daughter Freya, who taught me strength and courage. To my son Harry, who taught me wisdom. And to my niece Molly, who taught me commitment.

Praise for *The Gifts of Compassion*

"Compassion is one of the most courageous and wise of all our motives. Around the world, scientists are beginning to understand how it operates in our brains and in our bodies to produce wellbeing and pro-social behaviour. In this beautifully written book, esteemed clinical psychologist and therapist Stan Steindl takes us on a personal journey into the ups and downs of what it is to be human and reveals both the challenges and the joys of building one's compassionate mind."

Professor Paul Gilbert OBE, Founder of Compassion Focused Therapy and best-selling author

"Suffering is not our fault, but it is our responsibility. Fortunately, everyone has what it takes to alleviate suffering — compassion! Smart and engaging, this book unpacks the science of compassion in a delightful way and shows how to bring compassion into our lives when we need it the most. Don't miss the special topics on shame and forgiveness. Highly recommended!"

Dr Christopher Germer, Harvard Medical School.
Author, *The Mindful Path to Self-Compassion*

"This extraordinary book takes you in a fascinating journey from the depths of our human minds and the nature of suffering, through what compassion truly is and entails, towards how we can nurture, embody and manifest it in our lives in ways that are helpful to us and to others. The author is to be commended for this splendid book that skillfully takes the complex science of compassion and weaves it into a straightforward guide to personal practice. This book is a gem. A true gift and a 'must read' to all who want to experience and share the life-changing potential of compassion."

Dr Marcela Matos, University of Coimbra, Portugal

"Every human being suffers. For some, this suffering is overwhelming and impacts every aspect of their lives. As we now know from science, compassion towards self and others is the antidote. In *The Gifts of Compassion*, Dr. Steindl provides not only an understanding of the basis of suffering but a clear-cut path to overcome our suffering. His book is a gift to each of us."

James R. Doty, M.D., Stanford University Center for Compassion and Altruism Research and Education (CCARE)
Best-selling author of *Into the Magic Shop: A Neurosurgeon's Quest to Discover the Mysteries of the Brain and the Secrets of the Heart*

"This is an immensely readable book, grounded deeply in theory. Stan Steindl's deep understanding of the healing power of compassion emerges from years of working with others making the book both theoretically interesting and useful. With wisdom, compassion, and humor this book gives us an open door to live a more compassionate life."

Deirdre Fay, LICSW, Author of *Becoming Safely Embodied and Attachment-Based Yoga & Meditation in Healing Trauma*

"It's a real gift to be able to translate complex biosocial, psychological models of human functioning in a way that's accessible, practical, relatable and inspiring to us all. Dr Steindl has done exactly that in *The Gifts of Compassion* and this is what makes his book different. As a leading practitioner in compassion focused therapy, he has combined his theoretical knowledge and clinical skills with his gift for storytelling. His book is a joy; reading like a story, flowing through your mind and peppered with pearls of wisdom to help us all deal with life's struggles through the lens of compassion focused therapy."

Dr Deborah Lee, clinical psychologist and author of *The Compassionate Mind Approach to Recovering from Trauma: Using Compassion Focused Therapy*

"This book is rich with gifts that help address that which we all experience, suffering. Steindl takes us through clear, practical and personal examples of how Compassion Focused Therapy can help alleviate and prevent suffering. Excellent reading for anyone interested in compassion."

Dr James N. Kirby, Compassionate Mind Research Group, The University of Queensland

Contents

About the Author xiii
A note about *The Gifts of Compassion Personal Practice Workbook*............xv
Prologue xvii

Chapter 1: A Very Short Telling of a Very Long Tale 1

In the Beginning 1
The Human Brain: Seeking Safety from Threats 2
The Human Brain: The Drive and the Strive...3
More Compassion than Cruelty 4
We are not Zebras! 4
Our Caring Motivation 5
The Human Brain: To Affiliate and Belong 7
Assessing Your Three Emotional Systems 10
But the Brain is Very Tricky..10
Born to have Experiences 13
Not Your Fault..14
The Flow of Life 14
But it is Your Responsibility 15
Three Pearls 18

Chapter 2: What is Compassion?...19

A Compassionate Motivation 19
Setting a Compassionate Intention 20
Fears, Blocks and Resistances...21
Exploring Fears, Blocks and Resistances 23
Soothing the Fears 23
Beginning with the Body...25
Friendly Face, Friendly Voice 25
Breathing to Soothe 26
Soothing Rhythm Breathing 26
Safeness 28
A Definition of Compassion 29
The Three Flows of Compassion 30
Three Pearls 31

Chapter 3: A Deeper Dive into the Attributes of Compassion 33
The Attributes of Compassion 36
Sensitivity 36
Sympathy 36
Distress Tolerance..39
Empathy 41
Non-judgment 42
Care for Wellbeing 43
Practicing Compassion 44
Making a Commitment 45
Three Pearls 46

Chapter 4: Moving from What to How..47
Practicing Skills and Competencies 47
Attention 48
Imagery 48
Reasoning 49
Behaviour 51
Sensory 51
Three Pearls 52

Chapter 5: Mindfulness and Imagery, Attention and Safeness 53
Attention Training with Mindfulness 53
Mindfulness of Thoughts..55
Safety Versus Safeness 57
Safe Place Imagery 58
Three Pearls 60

Chapter 6: Compassionate Other, Compassionate Self..................61
Using Imagery to Create an Ideal Compassionate Being....................61
Going Deeper with the Ideal Compassionate Other 62
Relating to the Ideal Compassionate Other 63
Describing Your Ideal Compassionate Other 65
Compassion as a Brain Pattern 66
Compassion for Others 67
Lights, Camera, Action!..68
Beginning to Imagine Your Compassionate Self..................................69
Walking About as Your Compassionate Self 71
Using the Compassionate Self with a Life Difficulty 72
Three Pearls 74

Chapter 7: We are Made Up of Many Different Parts 75
Multiplicity, and Working with Multiple Selves 75
Understanding our own Multiplicity: Is there anything else? 83
When the Selves are in Conflict 84
Bringing the Compassionate Self to Emotional Integration 85
And So Begins the Conversation 91
Three Pearls 93

Chapter 8: Working with Self-Criticism 95
When the Critic Joins the Conversation 95
The Mixed Blessing of Self-Monitoring 97
The Elusive Ideal Self 98
The Different Forms of Self-Criticism 98
So, How Did Self-Criticism Evolve? 100
The Functions of Self-Criticism 100
The How and Why of Your Self-Criticism 101
But I DO Make Mistakes! 104
A Functional Analysis of Self-Criticism 104
Your Impressions of the Critical Self? 106
Cultivating Compassionate Encouragement 106
Your Impressions of the Compassionate Self? 107
Bringing Compassion to the Critic 108
Three Pearls 109

Chapter 9: Working with Shame 111
Introducing Shame 111
What do They Think, What do I think? 114
Getting to Know Our Shame 115
Active Shaming and Memories of Being Shamed 118
How Dare You Treat Me This Way! 120
But I Feel Bad About What I Did 123
Is it External Shame, Internal Shame, Humiliation or Guilt? 124
The Multiplicity of Self-Conscious Emotions 125
Bringing the Compassionate Self to Self-Conscious Emotion 127
So We Activate the Compassionate Self 127
Approaching the Self-Conscious Emotions 128
Three Pearls 130

Chapter 10: Forgiving You, Forgiving Me, and Having Healthy Relationships 131

What is Forgiveness, and What Isn't It? 131
Empathy as a Part of Forgiveness..133
Compassion for Others, Compassion for Self................................134
May I Begin to Forgive..135
A Letter of Forgiveness...137
When the Person We Need to Forgive is Ourselves 139
Setting Boundaries with Compassionate Assertiveness 140
Aggression, submission, or assertion?...142
Let's Assert!...143
Expressing Appreciation 143
Three Pearls 145

Chapter 11: Practical Strategies for Deepening your Compassionate Self........................147

Recapping the Core Principles 147
Breathing with Affection 149
Colouring to Compassion 150
Writing a Compassionate Letter to Yourself 151
Compassion in Your Pocket 152
Mirror, Mirror 153
Compassion in Daily Life 154
Three Pearls 160

Chapter 12: Where To From Here?...161

Pulling it all together… 161
Compassion is about Prevention 163
And Compassion is about Alleviating Suffering............................164
And Finally, Sending You Compassionate Wishes 164

Further Reading...167

About the Author

Dr Stan Steindl is a clinical psychologist in Brisbane, Australia. He is a director of the successful private practice Psychology Consultants Pty Ltd, as well as an adjunct associate professor at the School of Psychology, University of Queensland (UQ).

Stan has provided training and supervision in matters related to clinical psychology extensively in Australia over the last 20 years. He also has a strong interest in the science and practice of compassion, and the application of compassion in therapy and therapeutic relationships. He is the co-director of the UQ Compassionate Mind Research Group.

If you would like to stay in touch with Stan you can:

Follow him on Facebook:

https://www.facebook.com/drstansteindl/

LinkedIn:

https://www.linkedin.com/in/stan-steindl-150a5264/

Twitter:

@StanSteindl

Or hear more from Stan at his YouTube channel, *Stan Steindl, Compassion in a T-Shirt*:

https://www.youtube.com/channel/UCujCvGkc_TFF7KmA0Sk4E7A

A note about *The Gifts of Compassion Personal Practice Workbook*

You will notice throughout this book mention of: 'your *Personal Practice Workbook*'. This refers to the accompanying book — *The Gifts of Compassion Personal Practice Workbook* which is available for sale as a separate paperback. It follows the same chapter structure as *The Gifts of Compassion* but is designed to guide you further in your compassionate journey. The workbook provides you with the opportunity to think and reflect about your own life experiences and enhance the cultivation of your compassionate mind.

While there is much to be gained simply from reading *The Gifts of Compassion*, if you want to gain the most benefit from the knowledge, examples and practices covered, you may wish to also purchase the *Personal Practice Workbook*.

Each chapter of the workbook includes exercises and activities designed to deepen your understanding and practice of compassion for others, receiving compassion from others, and offering compassion to yourself and your own challenges and struggles.

Perhaps you can take it with you, as you continue on your compassionate journey!

Prologue

Suffering is a part of life.

I will help you develop strategies to make sure that sentence does not end there. In this book, you will be taken through a series of steps and practices specifically designed to minimise and overcome suffering.

As a human being, I'm used to dealing with my own anguish; as a psychologist, I'm also very familiar with the pain and struggle that others go through.

We are challenged in every aspect of our lives: intimate relationships are demanding, parenting is tough, and work can be problematic. Throughout our lives, there are periods when we fail, get sick or injured, grow old and lose the ones we love. Eventually, we face our own deaths as well.

Sometimes our problems are prompted by events outside our control — a sudden death, an accident, the unexpected loss of a job or the end of a relationship we value.

But more often than not, our suffering comes from within.

Worry and rumination, self-criticism and shame are just a few of the thought processes that humans possess, unlike any other living creature, that make us suffer.

We have a unique ability to keep the pain alive, long after and sometimes even long before, a distressing event has occurred.

For example, do you know the number of times you call yourself names in a day? I tried this experiment recently but gave up counting when I hit 27! On another occasion, I left the office for a break and when I reached the bottom of two flights of stairs, I realised I had forgotten my wallet. 'You idiot!' I said to myself under my breath, followed by the immediate realisation of just how unnecessarily harsh I was being on myself.

Critical self-talk is just one of the aspects of the complex human brain, and it's very common. It's also problematic because these thoughts fly just under the radar of our conscious mind — we're often quite unaware of what our brains are telling us. This condemning inner voice is also known to be related to common psychological difficulties, including anxiety, depression, stress, and shame.

All this begs the question, what can we do? How can we better manage the patterns of our tricky brains and instead of feeling anguish, flourish?

Well, the answer is already within us, deeply ingrained in our brains and in our essential being.

The answer is compassion.

Compassion is uniquely a human motivation. That's not to say that other animals, especially mammals, don't care for each other. They certainly do.

But among humans, it seems that our capacity for compassion goes a little further.

Like other mammals, especially those caring for their young, we possess that fundamental mammalian caring motivation, which is then supercharged by the social and emotional intelligence of the human brain, producing a compassionate motivation.

Compassion involves an awareness and sensitivity to the suffering of others, and of oneself, coupled with a desire and determination to try to help alleviate or prevent it. We can be aware of the distress of members of our family, our friends, our community, and even people on the other side of the world, and feel a motivation to try and help.

So, where does this compassionate motivation in humans come from and how can we harness it to alleviate our own anguish or help soothe the pain of other people?

To answer that, we need to go a long way back…

Chapter 1

A Very Short Telling of a Very Long Tale

In the beginning ...

Almost four billion years ago, long after the Big Bang, life on earth began to emerge. It began simply as single cells in a vast ocean, photosynthesis, carbon dioxide; then the cells started to make oxygen and eventually an ozone layer was created. The earth experienced an explosion of diversity, especially with respect to vegetation, and animals started to emerge in the seas and on the land. The first mammals appeared, and dinosaurs began to roam the earth less than 200 million years ago.

Then, 66 million years ago, another 'bang' resulted in a mass extinction killing three-quarters of all living creatures. However, this set the stage for a new era — over the next 50 million years mammals, including many of our most familiar animals, roamed the earth. Apes appeared 15 million years ago, and 200,000 years ago, the first people appeared.

Even the earliest humans looked a lot like us — and they had brains that functioned very similarly. It was the intricacies of their extraordinary brains which ensured the survival, against the odds, of our species.

Compared to other animals, humans aren't fast or strong. However, we can use our brains to assess danger and avoid predators: 'Hmm, last time I went over that hill, there was a lion. I wonder if there's one there now?'

The evolutionary dynamic is that animals adapt to protect themselves. Humans have done exactly the same thing.

Many of our greatest strengths as a species have emerged because of the wonders of our brains. However, these same mechanisms can also cause a lot of suffering.

My story

Throughout this book, you will find excerpts like this where I tell little stories of myself or people I know or have worked with over the years to illustrate certain concepts. Each excerpt will start with either 'My Story' or a person's name. The names and identifying information of the other people are changed for the sake of confidentiality, but my stories are basically true!

For example, I will never forget my first experience of learning compassion focused therapy (CFT) from the founder of CFT, Professor Paul Gilbert. It was at a workshop in Byron Bay, a beautiful seaside town in Australia. I remember listening to Professor Gilbert make the profound connection between psychology and evolution. Imagine that, a continuous flow of birth, survival, reproduction and adaptation — for millions of years. And the way we think, feel and act is designed *for* us over all that time, by all of that adaptation!

I remember thinking at the time that really, evolution is about survival and reproduction, and our brains are designed for this purpose. Evolution is not concerned with making us happy.

Of course, there are some ideas and practices that can help, and that's what this book is about!

The human brain: Seeking safety from threats

Our actions are still motivated by threat and drive systems. Our threat system arises from very ancient, even 'reptilian' neural structures such as the amygdala and limbic system which send out signals telling us 'It's better to be safe than sorry'.

This means our brains prefer to err on the side of mistakenly identifying a threat even when it is not there, rather than ever miss the presence of a threat that is there.

A number of bodily sensations are associated with the threat system: increased breathing rate, elevated heart rate, muscular tension, dry mouth, butterflies, nausea, shakiness, restlessness and a physical urge to act. Changes also occur in our attention; our focus becomes narrowed and we urgently scan our environment. The result, of course, is heightened vigilance, accompanied by anxiety and anger.

A number of behaviours are also exhibited as part of the threat system, including avoidance, submission, and aggression. This is commonly known as the fight/flight/freeze/appease response.

The human brain: The drive and the strive

Now, if the threat system had its way, then we would stay safe and warm in the cave. But we couldn't just stay in the cave! We had to go out and find the resources we needed to survive.

The *drive* system insists that we always 'strive for something better' including fundamental resources such as food, water, shelter, tools and sex. It also means striving for success and dominance and avoiding inferiority and shame. This system generally focuses on gratification for ourselves and those close to us and is accompanied by feelings of excitement and pleasure. Sometimes, this can lead to self-interest, selfishness or greed.

Although the threat and drive systems have some similarities in bodily sensations, such as an increased breathing rate, behaviourally the focus of the drive system is on seeking and acquiring. Rather than avoiding a real or imagined threat, the drive system motivates us to socialise, engage, acquire and celebrate.

Sometimes, the drive system feels a bit insatiable. The concept of *hedonic adaptation* relates to the idea that even when we finally get what we want, we tend to want more: the new smartphone, the bigger boat. This makes sense from an evolutionary perspective. We couldn't just go out and get one meal, and then rest on our laurels. We had to go out again and again, and the drive system motivates us to do that.

History is full of many examples of extraordinary human progress: the philosophies of the Ancient Greeks, the golden rule of religions, the age of enlightenment, the scientific revolution and the advent of democracy. But, despite so many advances, we still often feel, think and behave just like our ancestors from tens of thousands of years ago, those earliest Homo Sapiens, motivated by primitive systems of threat and drive.

More compassion than cruelty

The problem with the daily 'news' is that it's almost exclusively bad. It can appear that the world is in a constant state of competition, argument, conflict and war; anxiety and anger, greed and power seem to be at the heart of most conflicts.

Just think of people in peak-hour traffic. We've all seen footage of 'road rage' which can be a real problem with disastrous consequences. It grabs our attention. It can be easy to forget that most of the time we are all driving around following the rules, taking turns, cooperating and getting from point A to point B without any fuss. It's the same at a shopping centre where people politely queue up, or at work where people willingly collaborate to get a task finished. Despite some real problems, generally speaking, we are a very cooperative species.

We are not generally inclined towards killing each other. There are now well over 7 billion people on the planet and the fact that this number keeps climbing proves this. While cruelty and violence are certainly part of our basic nature, they do not loom large in most people's daily lives. The larger truth is that our basic disposition leans towards connection, relationship and cooperation, characteristics of our species not entirely explained by the threat and drive systems.

We are not Zebras!

Have you ever watched one of those wonderful David Attenborough documentaries? I'm sure you can imagine him in hushed tones describing the birth of a zebra foal. The newborn zebra struggles to her feet, wobbles a bit, maybe falls over, but within moments she's up, little tail wiggling cheerfully, and running with the dazzle of zebras. (Yes, you read that correctly — the collective noun for zebras is a 'dazzle'!).

That's how zebras survive — by being able to run from the moment they are born. Their survival relies on the threat system, and especially the flight response. If a predator approaches, even the youngest in the dazzle can flee.

When a baby human is born, however, they are, well, ... quite pathetic really! This might seem like a harsh word, but it means 'causing or evoking pity, sympathetic sadness, sorrow, etc.; pitiful; pitiable'. In a way, as we shall see, that's actually their superpower! Our babies are terribly vulnerable and remain so for a very long time. Sometimes they don't even leave home until well into their 20s!

Given the vulnerability of our young and the susceptibility of individual members of our species, we have needed far more than the threat or drive systems to keep us alive.

We needed a third system.

Our caring motivation

Our existence is not only governed by the instinct towards fight or flight, freeze or avoid, or our desire to obtain greater resources. We also have an innate motivation to care for each other, to soothe, nurture and cooperate.

All of this arises from the third system in the human brain, the *soothing system*, also known as the *affiliative system*. This is the system that motivates us to affiliate or connect with one another, to become families and tribes, and eventually towns, cities and nations. Human beings have always cared for our vulnerable — especially our vulnerable young, as well as our elderly, sick and disabled.

In anthropological research, scientists search for clues about human existence by examining the remains of people who lived tens of thousands of years ago. One significant finding has been the discovery of bones which show signs of chronic and disabling, but not necessarily fatal, medical conditions.

Such findings suggest that the sufferer could only have lived as long as they did due to the care and compassion of those around them.

While the earliest humans were arguably in danger from a scarcity of food, wild animals or natural disasters, the truth is they were most vulnerable when they were alone. Together, or as a group, we could probably fight off a lion, or deal with some other threat. Alone, we were dead.

Our species has evolved to work together as a group and protect each other. At our best, we nurture, comfort and soothe, and we possess an innate motivation to care for each other.

For example, imagine a little girl who you care about, and she's learning to ride a bike. The inevitable happens and she takes a small tumble. There she is, hurting, upset, suffering.

Your first instinct would be to approach her to check if she's been injured. If it's not too severe, you might offer some *physical comfort* like a reassuring hug. You might also say something to *validate* her suffering, *reassure* her that things will be okay, and *encourage* her to keep trying. And all the time you would be using a warm, caring and *friendly tone of voice*. You might even do something to be *helpful*, and certainly not to cause further harm.

We might say, in soothing tones, something like this:

> Ooh, that's a nasty one (validation). Come here and give me a cuddle (physical comfort). You'll be OK (reassurance). Here, let's put some ice on there (doing something to help). Come on, up you get, back on the bike (encouragement).

Keep these pieces in mind. I'll come back to them time and time again. Physical comfort, validation, reassurance, encouragement, friendliness, and helpfulness are key ingredients of the soothing system and ultimately key ingredients of *compassion*.

We survive by looking after each other. And, as we shall see later, we can also turn this motivation for caregiving, protecting, nurturing and encouraging towards ourselves.

The human brain: To affiliate and belong

Every one of us has the *soothing-affiliative system* as an integral part of our brains. This tendency towards forming cooperative relationships evolved to meet our need to survive by helping us to be open, calm and content; it can also regulate feelings of threat. This system forms the basis of our ability to empathise and sympathise and, as such, develop benevolent feelings towards others.

Soothing system activation is experienced in the body as groundedness, calmness, contentment, slowing and softening, as well as a sense of well-being. Our attention becomes more open, exploring, reflective, and helpful, and our behaviour becomes more peaceful, settled, gentle, friendly, and playful.

Our soothing system was developed as a part of our neural structures thousands of years ago and is a core aspect of our humanity. And, as we will see, it is a source of great compassion both for ourselves and others.

Now just bear with me while we delve into a little science. The soothing system is associated with neural structures such as the pre-frontal cortex, cingulate cortex and hypothalamic midbrain circuits. Several neural structures have been found to help us to connect with others and drive caregiving, nurturance, trust and safety. When our bodies release oxytocin, a hormone produced in the hypothalamus, it signals bonding and promotes trust and kindness.

The soothing system is also associated with the parasympathetic nervous system and the ventral vagal system. If the central nervous system were a car, then the sympathetic nervous system would be the accelerator, increasing the body's physiological responses. The parasympathetic nervous system would be the brake, helping to regulate our threat and drive systems.

And so, in order to activate our soothing system, we need to foster practices aimed at developing the parasympathetic system.

The vagal nerve, in particular, has been found to help with slowing down the heart rate, as well as having a tantalisingly important and complex role to play in social engagement, healthy attachments and a sense of personal safety within the group. The parasympathetic system and the vagal nerve help us to approach and affiliate with each other when we feel secure or when we need to feel safe.

To deliberately cultivate compassion for others, we need to bring this system to our conscious awareness and activate it. Importantly, this same system can be focused on our own needs so that we develop our ability to offer ourselves comfort in times of stress.

Joan

> As a therapist, one of the activities I do on a regular basis is run groups that are aimed at helping people cultivate their compassionate minds. One such group is designed to help people bring self-compassion to their own bodies. Many people struggle with body image shame. It is very painful and difficult to cope with, and there are many aspects of modern society (for example the fast-food industry and the diet industry) that give us all very mixed message about our bodies. Self-compassion can be a way to soothe our feelings of shame about our bodies and how we look.
>
> Joan was a participant in one of these groups. We had talked about the threat system, and she seemed very aware of this. She knew the fight/flight/freeze response and was aware that she was often highly threat activated. When we talked about the drive system, she noticed how so often she was high on drive, and further, that the drive system was a way to compensate for her ever-present threat system. So, much of the time, she experienced lots of threat and lots of drive.
>
> When we discussed the soothing system, she was absolutely taken aback! She knew she could soothe others; it was a big part of her job and she looked after people a lot. Her realisation was that she herself rarely, if ever, felt safe, settled, comforted or soothed. And it was a rather painful realisation, because as she said, 'Where do we learn to soothe ourselves? By being soothed. I was never really soothed when I was little.'
>
> The good news was that now she knew. She had learned about the soothing system, and the next steps were to develop it and learn practical ways to activate it whenever she needed it most.

By activating this soothing system and its related calmness and openness, we can:

1. Become more aware of others and ourselves in the world.

2. Understand each and every one of us as a whole person with our own histories and backgrounds, with idiosyncrasies and understandable quirks.
3. Begin to see that every person is just like us, and we are just like them. Sharing a common humanity, we all face the same primary challenges and deal with our own versions of suffering.

My story

The three emotional systems, threat, drive and soothing, are ever-present, always activated to a greater or lesser extent. We are never really in just one system, and the three systems fluctuate across time and across contexts. Monitoring these systems can be a really useful place to start, such that at moments throughout the day you can ask yourself, 'How threatened do I feel right now? How driven do I feel right now? How soothed do I feel right now?'

Right now, as I write this example, it is 10.30pm and I am getting ready for bed. I stop and reflect on these three emotional systems. On a scale of 0 to 10, I would say that my drive system is currently at about a 1. I'm a little tired after a busy and long day, and I am not feeling a lot of drive, excitement or motivation to pursue any kind of goal. I would say that my soothing system is currently at a 5. I do feel relatively calm and certainly safe and secure at home.

However, I notice a slightly elevated threat system! I am feeling heightened anxiety right now and apprehension. I can feel butterflies in my stomach and restlessness in my body. I would say that my threat system is currently at a 7 — not maxing out, but definitely up a bit. I realise that I have a big presentation to give tomorrow morning. It means a lot to me and I want to do it well. I'm worried that I am underprepared! And the anticipation of it just niggles at me. All this suggests that it might be time to do some meditation to help down-regulate the threat system.

This can be a useful practice: checking in with your three emotional systems, and giving them a rating out of 10, and then taking steps to keep the three systems in balance. More about how to do this will be discussed throughout this book.

Assessing your three emotional systems

How would you rate your three emotional systems right now? Spend a few minutes to pause and reflect on each system. If you like, you can go to your *Personal Practice Workbook* and colour in the bar graphs on page 3. Alternatively, simply make a few notes in a way that feels most comfortable to you.

So, on a scale of 0 to 10, decide how activated your threat system is, with feelings of anger, anxiety and/or disgust? Use a red pencil to indicate your current level of threat system activation.

How about your drive system? How activated is that feeling right now, in terms of your level of excitement, energy and drive? If you like, use a blue pencil to indicate your current level of drive system activation.

And finally, think about your soothing system, that state of feeling safe and secure, peaceful, calm, comforted, and free to explore the world. How activated is your soothing system right now? Use a green pencil to indicate your current level of soothing system activation.

You can do this exercise anytime. It's a great way to monitor yourself. We will be talking about these three systems throughout this book, so getting into the habit of reflecting on your own threat, drive and soothing systems now could be really useful going forward.

But the brain is very tricky

So far, so good. Our brains have been exquisitely developed to help us: survive, avoid harm, deal with a threat, seek food, sex and status, and soothe, nurture and look after one another. However, we also have a newer range of additional brain functions, which are both wondrously helpful and ponderously painful at the same time.

The human brain has developed several new functions, and it is also because of these, we have been successful as a species. The first is our ability to be *self-aware* and also aware of ourselves in a social context. It is through this consciousness that we have the ability to monitor ourselves, to notice our thoughts, feelings and behaviours. We also have the ability to *imagine*, not least being able to remember the past or envision the future, and as a result, we can analyse, problem solve, learn, invent, create, plan ahead and many other functions that have contributed to the progress of our civilisation. We can also imagine the minds and experiences of others, sometimes referred to as *mentalising*, how they might think, how they might feel, and what they might need. Our social intelligence and the ability to communicate have been integral to our surviving together.

However, these new brain functions come with some very problematic trade-offs.

For example, self-awareness can easily turn to self-criticism, which can be agonising, especially when the voice inside your head is hateful and unrelenting.

If you think of a dog, wagging her tail, eating, lazing in the sun and chasing pigeons, she's not thinking, 'Oh, I'm having such a bad hair day. I bet no-one likes me!' This ability to be self-aware, and then to condemn oneself seems to be unique to humans. Add to this mix social awareness, concerns about status, beauty or wealth and the self-criticism turns to feelings of shame. We will discuss self-criticism and shame in detail later, as well as ways to bring compassion to those panful aspects of how the human brain works.

Having an imagination comes along with consequences too. Often, we might envision the future, but in a way that expects the worst, or gnaws at us with 'what ifs'. Our ability to imagine can also turn into fearful fantasies, which leaves us with anxiety, worry and panic. 'What if I arrive at the party and everyone hates me and wishes I hadn't come?' Rarely do we imagine a positive response from others; we are far more likely to think others will evaluate us negatively, as unattractive and unworthy.

It's not only the future that is not safe from the critical mind; it's the past as well. Our brains can be very selective with our memories, focusing on only the negatives of an experience. This can be expressed as 'if only's'. 'If only I'd worked harder, then my colleagues would have liked me and I would have fitted in much better.' This becomes particularly difficult when we start to ruminate; going over and over negative instances and regrets. Often, we're not even conscious that we're doing it — we might not even be aware of these thoughts that can lead to sadness and depression.

We can get caught up in all sorts of difficult loops of the brain.

My story

> I was driving home from work the other night, and just as I was making my way across the bridge, I drifted too far to the right and had to quickly swerve back to my lane. In some ways this was a minor event. No one was coming the other way, I realised what was happening in moments, and I came back to my lane without incident. It was just a lapse in concentration.
>
> But this really began to trouble me. 'What if there had been a truck coming towards me? What if I had crashed and been injured? What if I had injured someone else, or someone was killed!? What if I had died? What happens after you die!?'
>
> It helped when I realised; this is what the human brain does.
>
> My old brain threat system was triggered by the experience itself, and then my new brain took over, taking the external experience and bringing it internally, and I started to imagine, remember, worry and ruminate. As far as I know, we are the only animal that wonders and worries about their own death, and what might happen after death.
>
> Our tricky brains really do cause us a lot of suffering.

And to make matters worse, our new brain gives us the ability to not only struggle with the things that are going on around us but also the things that are going on within us. We start to develop fear about our own negative thoughts and feelings. We try to push them away, avoid them, trying to cling instead to the thoughts and feelings we do like, getting ourselves tied up in cognitive and emotional knots. 'What if I always feel this way?' or 'If only I didn't have these thoughts.'

As you can no doubt start to see, the human brain can be quite problematic. We have very *tricky brains*! In fact, all of these functions are already there for us on the day we are born: threat, drive and soothing systems, self-awareness, imagination, anxiety, anger, sadness, self-criticism: it's all there in our evolved human brain, ready to help us survive, and also ready to cause us a lot of suffering.

But once we are born, what happens next? That is also important, as we shall now see.

Born to have experiences

We are born, quite by chance, into a certain body, with a certain brain, and a certain life. We have no say over our gender, race, culture, religion, society, economic status, geographic location or family. And it matters because these characteristics have a powerful effect on the life we go on to lead.

There are two sides to this. One is that we cannot take all the credit for any talents we possess, or successes we achieve. Of course, hard work and perseverance can be part of our success, but even these are qualities that might have been bestowed upon us by chance. It can be well-worthwhile seeing the privileges we have and making good use of them and being helpful to ourselves and others.

The other side is that we can't be blamed (or blame ourselves for that matter) for all our faults, flaws, disappointments and failures. We all can make poor choices, but scratch the surface and we usually find a personal history which explains our decisions. Of course, we want to do what we can to work with various aspects of ourselves that cause us problems, but without blaming or shaming ourselves for having those aspects in the first place.

I have been very lucky, really, for various aspects of my own upbringing. Had any part of my upbringing been different, I may have become a very different version of myself. During what was an emotionally painful Grade 11 at school, I was given a very special book by an older boy at the school. This set me on the path of becoming a therapist, even at that young age, and had that random event not happened, who knows who I might be right now!

Any of us are only one version of all the possible variations of ourselves we could have been, had we been born and raised in another time or place. Consider how we all have simply become one particular version of ourselves, having been born into a social context none of us gets to choose, in which life experiences simply start to happen, and start to shape us.

Not your fault

A lot of what you experience, even your worst thoughts, feelings, and behaviours, are *not your fault*. Yes, that's right:

It's not your fault.

There is a second part of this statement which we can consider in a moment, but it's really vital that you know that your suffering is not your fault. The brain is basically an organ, much like any other organ of the human body, and it produces urges, desires, motives, thoughts and emotions.

Here's a question: what is your next thought?

We never actually know what our next thought is going to be. Most thoughts simply come into our minds without any warning and are quite involuntary. What arises in us is not even really our choice, let alone our fault — this can be a difficult concept to understand or accept. The purpose of making it clear that the way you think and behave is 'not your fault' is to steer you away from the tendency to blame and shame, but in a way that involves mind awareness and reality checking.

We are born with genes we did not choose and a tricky brain that gets caught in loops, and we are then shaped by experiences that we also did not choose. The version of ourselves that we become is just one of many possible versions, and none of this is our fault.

The flow of life

Let's sit or lie back for a moment and slow everything down. Get yourself comfortable, open up your body, relax your shoulders, arms, legs, and take a few slow, soothing, calming breaths. Bring a friendly expression to your face.

When you are ready, see if you can bring to mind a sense of your family tree. People you may have known, and some you may not — your two parents, your four grandparents, your eight great grandparents. Consider too, other important people who have helped shape you, guided you, or offered life lessons.

Then bring to mind all your ancestors. Think about each generation that came before, who have lived all over the world, and met and loved one another for lifetimes, or for brief moments. Connect with the fact that you come from a long line of people, stretching back across the millennia.

Allow your mind to gently reflect all the way back to those earliest ancestors — individual humans who had thoughts and feelings, urges and motives, and made their way in the world and survived.

And continue to go back further through the living beings before that, that evolved over millions of years. Know that you are part of this flow of life. See if you can bring gratitude to each and every one of them and their contribution to who you are today.

You wouldn't be here without every last one of them. We wouldn't be who we are without every last one of our ancestors. All our good bits (and not so good bits) are thanks to them.

We are the current stewards of their legacy, and we will do our best while we are here with what we've got. Others may follow, and so the flow of life goes on.

But it is your responsibility

While a lot that goes wrong (and right, for that matter) is not our fault, the fact remains that our brains can be a source of suffering for ourselves and others.

So, while we try to steer ourselves away from blame and shame, we don't want to become either lax or indifferent, or despairing or disempowered.

Imagine a person who just needs to quickly duck into the shopping centre to get milk and bread, but there aren't any spaces left because it's just after school pick up. Feeling stressed and pressured, the person makes a split-second decision to take a disabled carpark space close to the entrance. 'I'll just be a few minutes,' they say to themselves as a justification.

While this scenario could turn out fine, it might be that a genuinely disabled person who uses a wheelchair arrives for an urgent medical appointment to get a script they desperately need. They cannot park. Unfortunately, the first person's decision to take the disabled space leads to obstacles and difficulties, and possibly danger and suffering, for the second person.

We do need to learn how to deal with the brain's outputs. In fact, we need to learn how to manage our brains just as we need to manage the other organs of our body. For example, our gut has outputs that can be rather unpleasant! And that's not our fault either; it's just how the gut works. So, we don't blame and shame ourselves about it, but we do need to find ways to deal with it hygienically. We use toilets and toilet paper, soap for washing our hands, and intricate sewerage systems to hygienically dispose of the gut's outputs.

With respect to our brains, we have a responsibility to learn and practice being 'psychologically hygienic'.

It really helps us if we learn about the brain, how it evolved over time, and how it works now. We can work towards developing our 'mind awareness', that is, becoming aware of our minds and what it is doing in any given situation. And with a compassionate intention, we can practice being aware and sensitive to our own and others' suffering, then take steps to alleviate or prevent that pain.

We have to take responsibility for what our brains and minds do, while at the same time not blaming, criticising, or shaming ourselves.

It's also important to realise that we have feelings, but we are not our feelings. We have thoughts, but we are not our thoughts. Feelings and thoughts come and go. Keep in mind this important catchphrase as you continue through this book:

It's not my fault, but it is my responsibility.

Sami

> I once worked with a man in his late 50's. Sami came along to see me after urging from his wife as he was drinking a lot, and finding it very difficult to quit. All too often, he was having angry outbursts, especially when he was drinking, but not exclusively. He would get angry, enraged, and then lash out at whoever was closest, usually his wife. Unfortunately, there was frequent yelling and screaming, punching walls, and throwing things.

Sometimes there was rough grabbing and pushing. By the time he came to see me, both Sami and his wife were at the end of their tethers.

Sami was very defensive and difficult to engage. I quite quickly could see that he felt terribly ashamed of who he had become, and yet he was also very sensitive to being criticised or judged. His anger seemed to burst forth out of humiliation. As we talked, and he began to feel safer in our working relationship, it became painfully clear just how much sadness was behind all this.

Sami had been a taxi driver for many years, and during this time he had experienced some very traumatic situations. The two most significant events were when he witnessed a fatal brawl outside a nightclub, and when he had hit and killed a young woman who had dashed out onto the road in front of him in an act of suicide. Even though neither event was his fault, Sami believed that somehow, he was to blame. 'I should have done more,' he would repeat to himself, over and over. His response may not have seemed either logical or rational but it was absolutely real for him and caused a great deal of suffering.

Sami had also experienced a tough, traumatic childhood. His father was a violent alcoholic, just as his father had been before him, and Sami recalled many shamings and beatings. Sadly too, his mother had been deeply affected by his father's violence and had become both physically and psychologically unwell. She died when Sami was 14 years old from breast cancer, and he blamed himself for all of this as well.

At one point I said, 'Sami, this is such a painful story. I really feel for you. You have suffered so much in your life. There you were, born into this world, and you didn't get to choose any of this. You didn't get to choose your brain for starters, and it sounds like there were some tricky genes there. And you didn't get to choose what was a really tough childhood, with violence and trauma. And the loss of your Mum. We can't help but be shaped by that sort of stuff. And then, even in adulthood, those traumatic experiences just happened out of the blue. They are awfully sad and tragic, and yet, it just seems so random for you to have to face those things.'

Sami paused. There was silence for a long while. At one point he said, 'Yeah.'

And then, after a little more silence he said, 'You know, a lot of what I do, a lot of who I am, it's really not my fault.' And at that point, he started to cry. Really cry. Sami sobbed for some time. We sat, and he cried until he gradually settled again then he looked right at me with conviction etched into his face.

'But I gotta change a few things,' he said. 'I don't want to treat my wife like that. I want to do better.'

'It's not your fault, and at the very same time, you'd kinda' like to take responsibility and make a change,' I said.

'Yeah,' he said.

Three Pearls

At the end of each chapter of this book you will be invited to reflect on *three pearls* from the chapter, in other words, three things that you would kind of like to remember, reflect a bit more on, or perhaps even put into practice in your daily life. This could be content from the book itself that you would like to remember. Or it could be practices or strategies that you would like to try. It could even be something that came to mind as you were reading that you would really like to think about some more. Really, this is just a chance to reflect on the book so far and see what you think.

So, reflect now on Chapter 1, and the very short telling of human history. And perhaps write down three pearls in your *Personal Practice Workbook*, or make your notes in some other way that feels comfortable to you.

Chapter 2

What is Compassion?

A Compassionate Motivation

So now you know a little more about the evolution of the human brain, the old and new functions. We have also talked about the role of social context and life experience, and how that can shape us. But there is also a unique motivation that emerges from all of these various aspects of what it is to be human — **compassion**.

This includes three flows of compassion: being compassionate *towards others*, being open to receiving compassion *from others*, and being compassionate *towards ourselves*.

We have the capacity to make the most of our mammalian caring motivation and bring to it the newer brain functions of social awareness and understanding. We also have the unique ability to take on the perspectives of others or, in other words, to put ourselves in their shoes. In doing so, we can set conscious, compassionate intentions towards alleviating or preventing suffering in ourselves and others.

But is compassion simply the same as kindness? Here are some examples of kindness:

- Remembering someone's birthday and bringing them a gift.
- Opening a door for someone or inviting someone to share your umbrella in the rain.
- Offering someone a place ahead of you in line or letting them merge in traffic.
- Giving someone a compliment, or telling them you appreciate their efforts.

These examples could be considered acts of kindness and the more of these, the merrier! However, compassion is a response to suffering, and its distinguishing features are:

- The wisdom and courage to notice, understand and approach suffering.
- The ability to remain calm, mindful, strong and grounded in the face of pain and distress.
- The desire, motivation and commitment to transform suffering.

As we proceed through this book, we will start to understand compassion and how to cultivate it.

So, I invite you to stop for a moment and think:

> What might it be like to bring more compassion into your life?
>
> How might you start to think and feel?
>
> Where might your attention be directed?
>
> What might you start to do differently?

Setting a Compassionate Intention

Every day we come into contact with family, friends, colleagues, and strangers, either in person, on the phone or via social media. And among all those people there might be someone who is vulnerable, suffering, or who might need our help.

And what a privilege it is, to be offered the opportunity to help someone! We can open ourselves up to the motivation to help people who are suffering, creating a compassionate intention. This compassionate intention can be expansive, including all human beings and living creatures, and then perhaps we can also start to include ourselves, offering ourselves compassion when we too feel vulnerable, or we struggle or suffer.

With awareness and intention, we can deepen our commitment to helping alleviate and prevent suffering in others, ourselves, and the world. It's no small task. It takes a lot of practice. But just imagine, what would it be like to have such a compassionate intention? What might you feel, think, say or do? How might you get started?

Fears, Blocks and Resistances

Fearing change, setting up mental blocks or resisting a new path is completely normal. So, it's important to immediately consider and explore any fears of compassion we might have.

Do we worry that being compassionate towards others will make us weak and people will take advantage of us? Do we feel we don't deserve to receive compassion from someone else? Or do we worry that being compassionate to ourselves is selfish or self-indulgent?

There can be many thoughts and feelings which block us from giving and receiving compassion. Often these responses stem back to early life experiences, and we may not even be consciously aware of them. Still, it is important to try to work through and find peace about early life experiences in order to feel safe and comfortable to cultivate compassion.

Human beings have an innate motivation to give and receive care, and it is from this primitive motivation that compassion has emerged. Our experiences as children shape the way we feel about people and relationships — these events or encounters also become embedded as emotional and relational memories and we are then conditioned to respond to others and ourselves in particular ways.

Remember Pavlov's dogs? Around the turn of the last century, a Russian physiologist, Pavlov, was measuring how much saliva dogs produced when presented with food. Quite by accident, Pavlov realised that if the food was presented at the same time as ringing a bell — normally a neutral stimulus to a dog — then gradually the bell on its own could trigger the dog to salivate. While it was natural for a dog to salivate in response to food, doing so in response to a bell meant that the dog had been *classically conditioned*.

We can also be classically conditioned to stimuli. A common example is when we hear a song which played at a significant moment in our lives — hearing the music reminds us of the experience and evokes the emotion we felt at the time. A song might make us feel happy, sad or angry, depending on the type of experience with which it has become associated. I heard *Push It* by Salt-N-Pepa on the car radio the other day and felt like I was 17 again! What songs do that for you?

However, sometimes, as children, we may have had difficult or traumatic experiences with our parents or caregivers; being frightened, hurt, abused or shamed can condition us to feel uncomfortable about close relationships as adults. We might learn that such attachments are a threat — even when someone is trying to be kind, helpful or caring, we can feel afraid. Or we might believe we are unworthy or undeserving of love, which can also be very challenging.

Many of us have an experience of shame from early in our lives. If this experience was traumatic, it is more likely to become part of our self-identity. Deep memories associated with humiliation and fuelled by shame often cause people to struggle to be compassionate to others, and to receive compassion from others or, for that matter, from themselves.

My Story

> A dear friend of mine, and colleague at the University of Queensland, is clinical psychologist and researcher, Dr James Kirby. James has contributed wide-ranging research into compassion, spanning child development, compassion in parents and teachers, the neuroscience of compassion and compassion-based interventions. But he also studies fears of compassion.
>
> He was the lead author on a recent paper that looked at fears of compassion and the relationship between those fears and a range of psychological outcomes. The results were striking. Fears of being compassionate towards others, receiving compassion from others and self-compassion were all significantly correlated with overall mental health difficulties. The strongest relationships they found were between fears of receiving compassion from others, and fears of self-compassion, with shame, self-criticism and depression.

Given all this, it is important to understand that many people will struggle with the idea of compassion across each of the three flows. However, equally important is the finding that these fears can make it more likely for people to experience emotional difficulties, not least shame, self-criticism and depression. And so often, this is where we start. Understanding these fears, blocks and resistances, where they might come from, and how to soften them so that we feel safe and willing to bring more compassion into our lives.

Below are examples of common fears, blocks and resistances to compassion across the three flows. What are your reservations about compassion? What might inhibit giving and receiving compassion for you? Your *Personal Practice Workbook* offers space for you to explore your own fears, blocks and resistances and write down your thoughts.

Exploring Fears, Blocks and Resistances

Fears
Compassion will make me weak or vulnerable. People will take advantage of me and my compassion. Being compassionate towards myself will expose me too much to painful feelings and will just make me feel worse.

Blocks
I don't know how to be compassionate. I never know what to say to be compassionate. I really don't deserve compassion. I should be compassionate towards others, but being compassionate towards myself is too self-indulgent.

Resistances
Compassion is stupid, foolish. It's dog-eat-dog out there, and you need to be tough. I'm not one of those silly do-gooders. I don't want to sit around with a bunch of hippies complaining about how awful things are. It feels too much like self-pity.

Soothing the Fears

It might seem counter-intuitive that giving or receiving compassion, including self-compassion, would activate the threat system. But consider the role of classical conditioning and the fact that we create certain early associations with compassion, and it does make a lot of sense. It makes sense, and it's not your fault.

There are a number of things to keep in mind as you approach the fears, blocks and resistances that might emerge as you go on to cultivate compassion.

1. There's no need to rush into this. Cultivating a compassionate mind is a bit like wearing in a new pair of boots. Try it on, wear it around for a bit, take it off, try it on again, but take your time and let it feel more comfortable and more familiar.

2. Remember that fears, blocks and resistances to compassion are probably stemming from old brain systems, especially the threat system. And that's okay. The threat system is designed to keep you safe, and it errs on the side of better to be safe than sorry.

3. Remember, too, that the new brain functions probably have an influence: remembering the past, imagining the future, seeing worst-case scenarios, worrying, ruminating, self-criticising. All of this is completely normal, and so we can watch out for the way these new brain functions can loop back and further activate the threat system.

4. Don't forget that life experiences can influence how we feel about compassion as well. Difficult experiences with attachment figures of caregivers can make us feel very wary of others getting close or offering help. Caring can get confused with threat. But other aspects of experience can be relevant too, such as culture, social norms, peer groups and so on.

5. And always remember that none of this is your fault, it's just how the human brain works. It's tricky, and even something like compassion can be tricky too. So, as strange as it sounds, we can start by bringing a little bit of compassion to our own fears, blocks and resistances to compassion. Maybe even just start there.

However, to cultivate compassion for others and ourselves, we first need to soothe this threat-based fear of compassion. And so, we must go back to basics.

Beginning with the Body

Certain body postures result from certain emotional states: we might cower with fear, or bow our heads and slump our shoulders when we're sad. But it is also true that consciously changing our posture can change our emotional state.

It's important to become fully aware of posture so right now, notice how you are holding yourself. Begin to develop body awareness and intentional posturing to develop a sense of calmness, confidence, and safeness.

A compassionate body posture means having your head up, eyes facing forward to the horizon, your neck straight, and your shoulders back and chest open. This creates openness, rather than the narrowly focused attention of the threat system. It also opens the diaphragm, which can further assist the parasympathetic nervous system.

Try it now. Sit up so your body is in an upright but relaxed position. Lift your shoulders, roll them back, and then let them drop. Notice the feeling as your chest opens up. Be aware that your head is slightly lifted and with your eyes open you may now observe the world.

Friendly Face, Friendly Voice

Another integral aspect of compassion is the ability to cultivate an attitude of warm friendliness. We are a particularly social species; we are very sensitive, even vigilant, to the tiny movements on people's faces in an effort to understand how they might be feeling. Tone of voice matters too, with even minimal vocal bursts conveying every emotion from delight to disgust.

Try a neutral facial expression for a few seconds, and then a friendly look. This might include smiling, relaxing your jaw, softening your expression, even slightly raising your eyebrows. You could then experiment with an angry face with furrowed brow and clenched jaw. Notice how different each expression makes you feel.

To achieve a friendly tone of voice, imagine greeting a dear friend, and say hello to yourself in a way that feels genuine and warm. 'Hello [say your name].' Combine this with a cheerful smile. This might feel quite odd, but it will help you become aware of your usual facial expressions and voice tones so you can consciously shift these towards warmth and friendliness, which can add to your compassionate intention.

Breathing to Soothe

What's the first thing you do when someone approaches you unexpectedly from behind and speaks abruptly? You have a sudden intake of breath which brings in oxygen to start the heart pumping and send adrenalin around the body to fuel the muscles.

There has been a lot of research into the central role the breath plays in physiological arousal. Put simply, the faster the breath, the greater the fear. So, one simple yet powerful strategy to activate the soothing system is to do the opposite and bring a slow, soothing rhythm to your breath.

Let's bring the pieces together: posture, facial expression, voice tone and soothing rhythm breathing.

Soothing Rhythm Breathing

Firstly, sit comfortably with your feet flat on the floor. Make your back straight but relaxed, open your chest, and let your shoulders drop. You want to achieve a physical state that is laid back but aware.

Bring your attention to your breath. Notice your chest gently rising and falling as you breathe in and out; become aware of whether the air is cool on your nostrils or upper lip as you breathe in. Let the breath fill your lungs, and feel your chest and diaphragm rise. Then allow it to fall gently out through your nostrils — notice if it feels just that little bit warmer.

Without using too much control, allow your breathing to slow down, to deepen and lengthen. When you are ready, see if you can breathe in for a count of three and out for a count of three. As you breathe out, just let go of any tension or uneasiness. Continue like this for several moments.

Next, slowing your breathing rate a little more, breathing in for a count of four and out for a count of four. Bring your attention once again to your facial expression. Relax your brow and jaw and bring an almost imperceptible smile to your face. Continue breathing at this rate for several moments.

And next, slowing your breathing rate a little more, breathe in for a count of five now and out for a count of five. Start to say, silently in your own mind, and with a warm, friendly voice tone, 'mind slowing down, body slowing down'. Each phrase can be said on the out-breath, slowly, calmly, and with a friendly voice.

As you observe your natural breathing rhythm, become aware of its effects. The key is to breathe in and out, gradually finding the soothing rhythm that activates that parasympathetic nervous system.

You may find your mind starts to wander, and that's perfectly okay. Just notice it, then gently guide your attention back to the breath.

Continue practising this soothing rhythm breathing.

Kristiana

> When I saw Kristiana's name in the diary, I was excited to see her. We had previously worked together extensively, managing anxiety and some difficult distress that anxiety had been causing her. Using a compassion-focused approach seemed to be very helpful, and we had concluded our work together around the same time as she had fallen pregnant with her first child. A year or two later, we met again for a follow-up.
>
> As Kristiana was describing her experiences with the birth a little smile came to her face and she said, 'I think you'll appreciate this.' I was very curious about what she might be about to say! She went on to describe how, in the middle of all the action in the birthing suite, she had required emergency intervention by the doctor. This had been terribly frightening for her, and she felt close to panic. What was happening? What was going wrong? Was her baby okay?
>
> Her husband tried to talk to her and distract her as the doctor was doing his work, but Kristiana felt this wasn't helping at all. She told him to stop talking (I'm not sure exactly how she might have phrased that to him), and just at that moment a little voice came to mind and said, 'Bring your attention to your own breath.' She closed her eyes and tried to focus on her breath, slowing down the in-breath and breathing slowly and smoothly out.
>
> Of course, doing Soothing Rhythm Breathing in this way doesn't take away anxiety; it didn't work like taking medication. But Kristiana

described how she was able to settle just a little, enough to get through the doctor's intervention, and the rest of the birthing experience went very well, resulting in a healthy baby boy.

Safeness

Challenging experiences of shame or trauma can shape how we feel about relationships, giving and receiving care, and cultivating compassion. Equally, early experiences of warmth and safeness can have a powerful effect.

Where do we learn to soothe? Often it is from being soothed by someone else. This might be a parent, of course, but sometimes people may have had more difficult experiences with parents. Sometimes soothing might come from a grandparent, someone with whom we always felt safe, loved, looked after and secure. Or it might be another family member — that one aunt who really took an interest. Or a teacher or coach who valued what we were doing. It might even be a family pet, such as the family dog who followed you everywhere you went and was there with you when you were having a tough time.

It can be wonderful to identify such a person or some other living being. For some, this is very difficult to do, and in that case, it is important to explore other ways to access that feeling of safeness and security. There is definitely more than one way to do it. However, oftentimes people can bring to mind someone or something that is associated with these feelings of belonging, soothing and care.

Consider now:

> Who do you remember feeling safe and secure with? (Consider family, friends, teachers, coaches, mentors, and even pets.)
>
> If that's not possible what about a piece of music, song or character in a book? Or is there a singer or someone famous who evokes these feelings in you?
>
> See if you can identify early memories of warmth and safeness.

We have an innate caring motivation which has been vital to the survival of our species. From this emerges compassion. However, when we are born, events and experiences shape the openness we feel towards being compassionate towards others, receiving compassion, and giving compassion to ourselves. Let's take a look at what compassion really is, and then in the next chapter we will explore the attributes that make up a compassionate person.

A Definition of Compassion

'Compassion' is derived from the Latin derivatives *com* 'with, together' and *pati* 'to suffer'. So, one translation or interpretation of the word 'compassion' might be 'to suffer with'.

Professor Paul Gilbert, a UK clinical psychologist who has worked extensively in understanding and cultivating compassion, has developed the following definition:

> Compassion is the sensitivity to suffering in self and others, with a commitment to try to alleviate and prevent it.

Professor Gilbert's definition helps us to understand the two main aspects of a compassionate motivation: the ability to notice and engage with suffering, and the desire or motivation to take action to alleviate and prevent it.

We can sometimes go through life on autopilot. We can be preoccupied with identifying threats and reacting to them; at other times, we might be more focused on our own drives for achieving or acquiring. It's also important to be alert to the times when we may be unaware of or oblivious to suffering. Compassion, which is the opposite to indifference, invites us to step out of autopilot, and notice the suffering around us or within us.

Awareness of suffering is the first step, but sometimes this can create such overwhelming feelings that we choose to avoid having to deal with it. So, compassion also asks that we cultivate the virtues of wisdom and courage: having the astuteness and emotional intelligence to know what to do, and the fortitude to do it.

Compassion, sensitivity and commitment:

> I'm really suffering right now. This situation is hard and painful. I really want to take steps to do something that might make things a little easier. What's something I could do right now that would be helpful for me and most supportive of my own wellbeing?

The Three Flows of Compassion

Compassion flows in three directions: compassion for others, receiving compassion from others, and offering compassion to ourselves, also known as self-compassion.

It's not always easy to achieve this third flow of self-compassion.

Compassion for others has been found to have a twofold benefit: it helps the person to whom compassion is being offered, and it benefits the person making the offering. However, being compassionate can become very fatiguing if you do not allow yourself to receive from others. In this instance, it's important to acknowledge that some people feel uncomfortable receiving compassion, despite feeling very comfortable giving it.

Perhaps we can consider compassion as the same energy that can flow in and out, for you and for me, so that we are receiving as well as giving.

Many professions are compassionate by their very nature: doctors, nurses, therapists, and paramedics, just to name a few.

Unfortunately, if we surveyed those same professionals, we would likely discover that they have lower scores on openness to receiving compassion from others and self-compassion than being compassionate towards others. Fears, blocks, and resistances to receiving compassion, either from others or from oneself, are often very prominent and difficult to shake.

However, as Jack Kornfield, a famous Buddhist psychologist, says: 'If your compassion does not include yourself, it is incomplete.' So, we develop an ability and willingness to open ourselves up to receiving compassion, including directing our own compassion, that same compassion that we might even offer another person, to ourselves when we too suffer.

Student Nurses

> One of the great privileges in my working life is to teach others about compassion! I get to speak to all sorts of people, but one group that I have often worked with is nurses. And actually, they have taught me a lot in return!

I remember working several years ago for the first time with a large group of student nurses. They were of all ages really, although a number of them were in their early twenties. They had nearly finished their training and were about to embark on their wonderful careers. Towards the end of their training, they were offered my course, which was called 'The Compassion Invitation: Exploring the Science and Practice of Compassion.'

As part of my course, I asked all the students to complete a questionnaire which assessed their levels of compassion according to the three flows: compassion for others, receiving compassion from others, and self-compassion. As you might expect, their scores on compassion for others was very high, much higher than those scores normally found in the general population. And, of course, nursing is one of the most compassionate jobs that there is!

But what was striking was just how low they scored on both receiving compassion from others and self-compassion. On these two flows, they scored lower than the general population. In fact, many of these nursing students were much more likely to be self-critical about their own suffering, and hide it away from others for fear of being judged as weak or incompetent. The significant implication there was that, given how tough it can be to work as a nurse and all the suffering that patients are going through, only being compassionate towards others and not receiving any compassion for themselves put them at risk of burnout and fatigue.

Being able to understand this idea of the three flows of compassion, and finding balance amongst those three flows, became an important point of discussion and provided a great place to start preparing for their own self-care moving forward to starting their careers.

Three Pearls

Once again, take a moment to reflect on Part 2 and the discussion so far about what is compassion. See if you can write down three pearls, three things that you would kind of like to remember, reflect a bit more on, or perhaps even put into practice in your daily life. Space is provided for your notes in your *Personal Practice Workbook*.

Chapter 3

A Deeper Dive into the Attributes of Compassion

Wisdom

Compassion is wisely assessing and understanding a situation in which another person, or ourselves, may be suffering, and then arriving at a course of action to help alleviate that suffering.

Wisdom is our ability to think and act using what we have learned through education, instruction, and life experience. It incorporates our ability to understand the complexities and nuances of a situation and draw on our *commonsense* and insight. Having wisdom means we approach a situation from a big picture perspective with a calmness and presence of mind necessary to identify and take skilful action.

In the context of compassion, the role of wisdom is to have a deep understanding of our evolved human nature. Many of our brain functions pose problems for us, including contributing to our own suffering. Wisdom helps us understand how to manage these functions, and accept they are part of the universal human condition. We just find ourselves here, in the evolutionary flow of life, with tricky brains we didn't choose and shaped by experiences we also didn't choose. And much of what we endure is not our fault.

Strength

> Compassion is...
>
> ...being strong, solid, and grounded, preparing the body and the mind to be in the presence of suffering, with dignity, fortitude, and perseverance.

Compassion requires a lot of inner *strength*, or in other words, a sense of being grounded and secure. Imagine you are standing waist-deep at the surfing beach. With each wave, you wriggle your feet a little deeper in the sand, lean forward a little and ready yourself for the next one. When the waves are smaller, you can relax, but as the swell grows and the incoming waves get larger, you need to strengthen your stance, stand firm and dig a little deeper with your feet.

In the context of compassion, strength begins with the body. We need to find a posture that feels well-anchored, well-supported, and grounded, a position that is upright, but relaxed. With this strength comes a sense of authority, dignity, as well as calmness and friendliness. There is no anger or impulse to fight or lash out, but rather a kindly strength.

Courage

> Compassion is...
>
> ...courageously persisting in approaching suffering, even when we feel fear, hesitation or urges to avoid, and taking the actions we wisely know will help to alleviate and prevent suffering.

Compassion is also aided by *courage*. It can be scary to approach suffering or to sit in its presence, whether that be another's suffering or our own. The most common barrier to compassionate action is fear. Sometimes when we begin to work towards living more compassionately various blocks can arise, such as low confidence, self-consciousness, vulnerability, anxiety and fear. But that's okay. Our wisdom tells us that this is part of what it is to be human. And very little in life that is important is going to happen easily.

Compassion does not require us to become fearless, but having courage means taking action even in the face of fear. Having courage means we persist with our willingness to approach the suffering of others and ourselves, in the face of fear and despite it. Of course, we should feel anxious and scared. We are human, after all.

This courage, and the strength and authority that goes with it, arises out of wisdom and clarity. When we truly embrace the wisdom of what it is to be human, and how it is that we suffer, then we can be steeled by this sense of responsibility and determination to help ourselves and others suffer less. Beginning with compassionate intention, grounding ourselves with posture, facial expression, voice tone and soothing rhythm breathing, we can connect with the courage and strength necessary for compassion.

Commitment

> Compassion is…
>
> …a commitment to be helpful, rather than harmful, to myself and others.

Being motivated by compassion involves a strong element of *commitment* to building the courage we need to turn towards, rather than away from, suffering.

We need a commitment to developing wisdom and courage. It can be very easy to ignore or avoid the suffering of oneself or others, and it can be very tempting to turn away when we do see it. But being committed to noticing suffering and trying to be helpful brings compassion to the fore of our minds, and opportunities to be helpful are more likely to be noticed and acted upon.

We can commit to developing the attributes and competencies for cultivating the compassionate mind, and we can commit to building ourselves into people who want to avoid causing harm to ourselves and others, and instead seek opportunities to be helpful.

The Attributes of Compassion

Let's now explore in more detail the key attributes of a compassionate person, also known as the first psychology of compassion, allowing us to engage with suffering.

The attributes of compassion are like building blocks; each can be considered and developed mindfully. You will find that some attributes you possess are more developed than others, so cultivating compassion will mean selectively working on the key attributes for you.

The six attributes of compassion, first proposed by Professor Paul Gilbert in his groundbreaking 2009 book *The Compassionate Mind*, are as follows:

Sensitivity

Sympathy

Distress Tolerance

Empathy

Non-Judgment

Care for Wellbeing

When these building blocks are well developed, they offer a foundation for compassionate action. Understanding their importance and developing your competence and mastery of these attributes will help you approach suffering in a skilful and confident way.

Now let's look at the six attributes in more detail. Consider each one, and then reflect in writing how you might further cultivate them.

Sensitivity

We are often preoccupied with the past and the future; most of us have little awareness of our present moment reality.

We all create stories in our minds about events and experiences, and these narratives are repeated over and over. Our brains focus on how everything is versus how everything should be, and then we struggle with the reality of life when the fantasy does not match up.

Rumination and worry can plague us, and we react with behaviours that are driven by craving and desire, escape and avoidance. We reach for food, wine, smartphones, television; there are so many ways we can distract ourselves from the suffering around and within us. Routinely diverting our attention from suffering often has the effect of making the situation worse.

Cultivating sensitivity involves openness, awareness and attention. Practising sensitivity often involves setting a purposeful intention at the start of the day (and then reminding ourselves at frequent intervals) to be present and aware, noticing disappointment, discomfort, pain and suffering.

You might even use a mantra such as:

> Today I will practice sensitivity.
>
> Today I will be aware of the interconnectedness of people, life and the universe.
>
> Today I will be sensitive to the hardship or suffering of others and myself.
>
> Today I will look for opportunities to be kind, helpful and compassionate.

Self-Reflection on Sensitivity

Take about five minutes to think about what you would like to do to develop sensitivity, or ways that you would like to be more sensitive. See if you can brainstorm three specific actions you could take to develop your sensitivity towards the suffering of others and yourself, and then write them down in your *Personal Practice Workbook*.

Sympathy

Compassion involves feeling concern, warmth and care for the person suffering, as well as experiencing and expressing sympathy.

Sometimes people feel cautious about being sympathetic as it can so often be mistaken for pity, which can leave a person feeling inferior or disempowered. Pity, however, involves feelings of contempt or scorn for the person suffering, a sense of superiority over them, or viewing them as powerless or pathetic. Sympathy, on the other hand, broadens our approach so that we see the other person's suffering, as well as their courage and endurance. Having sympathy means we are genuinely *moved* by the person's suffering and therefore are more motivated to help.

Similarly, taking a more sympathetic approach to ourselves when we suffer is not the same as self-pity. People often feel concerned not to wallow in self-pity, but sympathy in the context of self-compassion means we can be warmer, more caring and less self-critical. We can soften, and when we are moved by our own suffering and feel care and concern, we can also be motivated to offer ourselves kindness, soothing and care.

Sympathy — feeling moved emotionally by our own or another's suffering — is the motivational bridge from the awareness of suffering to compassionate action.

It might sound something like this:

> I am aware of this person's suffering. I feel sad and sorry that they are having this experience. I understand how painful it must be for them. I know I am not to blame for their suffering, and nor do I have the power to stop it. However, I care for this person's wellbeing. I'm concerned for them, and I want to try to do what I can to help them.

Jenny

> When I first mentioned the attribute of sympathy to Jenny, she had a very strong negative reaction towards it. She'd had a difficult upbringing in a family who didn't have a lot of money or resources and really battled along through life from one pay-cheque to the next. One of her mother's favourite sayings was, 'No point crying over spilt milk,' and when we explored that further, we discovered that it was often said forcefully, or even angrily. Whenever Jenny got upset, her mother would respond angrily with this kind of phrase and reject those feelings. Suffice to say that Jenny learned from a young age not to get upset.
>
> Unfortunately, things continued to be tough for Jenny, who went on to struggle financially in adulthood as well. She married a man when she was very young who shortly after that was drafted into the military and

sent to war. He came back a very different person to the one she had married, but she stuck with it, knowing that there was 'no point crying over spilt milk.' Over many years the couple struggled along. Her husband's drinking increased, he started gambling, and she looked after the kids until they had grown up. Now the couple were financially very badly off and she had come along to see me because of her own problems with anger and depression.

The idea of sympathy, especially feelings of sympathy towards herself, just seemed too soft and weak, patronising, and too much like self-pity. She really riled against the idea of self-pity.

So, we talked through all that she had been through, the blows she had been dealt, the way that none of this was her fault yet she had been through so much suffering. Quietly and gently, she started to feel sorrow for the little girl she had been, unable to get upset, and yet often feeling upset inside herself. And we started to bring into the light what it was like for her as an adult too, with all the struggles and traumas that were in her life. At a certain point, and it surprised us both, she started to cry. A little tear rolled down her cheek, and she said, 'I just feel so sad about all I have gone through.'

This is the kind of sympathy that helps cultivate a self-compassionate motivation.

Self-Reflection on Sympathy

How might you develop your sympathy for those who are suffering, including yourself? Spend about five minutes brainstorming three specific actions you could take in your daily life to develop sympathy. Write down your thoughts in your *Personal Practice Workbook*.

Distress Tolerance

Suffering is difficult. The reality of our human experience is that we all experience anguish and distress, and sometimes, we can be deeply affected by the pain of others. As Paul Gilbert has said, 'To be compassionate is to descend into the reality of the human experience.'

Think of Mother Teresa as she worked among the poor children and the dying of Calcutta. It must have taken enormous strength to manage the difficult feelings that would have arisen in the face of such tremendous hardship and distress.

As we cultivate more compassion, we must also fortify ourselves to be in close, intimate contact with suffering; like Mother Theresa, we need strength and resilience to maintain a compassionate life. We need to develop the attribute of distress tolerance.

The seemingly simple practice of using the breath to ground, steady and soothe punches well above its weight. This one technique allows us to let go of painful thoughts, sit with difficult feelings, and change the state of our parasympathetic nervous system. Deep, attentive breathing allows us to feel physiologically calmer in terms of our breathing rate, heart rate, blood pressure and muscular tension.

Self-compassion, while you are trying to help another person, is also vital; being compassionate to others without appropriate self-care can lead to fatigue and burnout. That may also mean you allow others to care for you when you need it. We try to maintain balance in the three flows of compassion. There is no doubt about the value of our social connections; we are hardwired to look after one another.

Self-compassionate coping means softening and soothing self-talk:

> I'm feeling distressed and upset right now, trying to work with this suffering. Suffering is a part of life. Everyone can feel this way and it is understandable that I should feel this way sometimes too. What do I need right now to soften my feelings and alleviate my own distress and suffering?

Self-Reflection on Distress Tolerance

What can you do to develop your ability to tolerate distress? What are three specific strategies you could use to develop your ability to tolerate distress in yourself or others? These are not easy questions to answer, however, write down your thoughts now in your *Personal Practice Workbook* and more ideas will be presented throughout the rest of this book.

Empathy

Empathy is a uniquely human ability to understand the feelings and meanings of another person.

One element of empathy is its *cognitive* component which allows us to imagine what an experience might be like for another person; to take their perspective and use language to describe their emotional state. However, empathy also runs much deeper into a heartfelt *affective* state where not only do we understand another person's emotional experience, but we can allow that feeling to resonate within us.

Empathy is knowing and feeling, understanding and experiencing, being aware of and resonating with the thoughts, feelings, motivations, intentions and meanings of another person. Empathy is also the ability and practised skill of conveying that understanding so that the other person also feels more understood.

But empathy is complex, and one person's empathy for another person's feelings is rarely, if ever, perfectly accurate. It varies depending on who the person is and their circumstances, who we are and the life experiences we have had, and many other factors. To say, 'I know exactly how you feel,' is not empathy as it's always an approximation of how the other person truly feels. Prematurely jumping to conclusions about another person's experience is the enemy of empathy.

Empathy is like an organism that shifts and grows through time, space, observation and conversation. The incisiveness of our empathy is served by observing and listening to the other person, reflecting on what they do and say, offering our impressions about what they may feel and mean, and being guided by them and their responses as we strive for an understanding of their world view.

And it is important to be able to bring empathy to ourselves so that we look carefully and wisely at the many emotions that we may be experiencing. And when we are distressed, it is our empathy which sees and understands our own feelings.

When difficult emotions arise, try to bring empathy to your experience:

What am I feeling right now?

How might this feeling have arisen?

In what ways might this feeling make sense in the context of my whole life?

Self-Reflection on Empathy

Spend a few minutes reflecting on empathy and write some notes in your *Personal Practice Workbook* about what you would like to do to develop your ability to empathise and understand others, or yourself, who may be suffering. Make a note of three specific actions you could take to develop your ability to empathise.

Non-Judgment

Non-judgment involves setting aside our assumptions and preconceived ideas and instead, opening our heart to the common humanity of all people.

Our genes and the environment we've grown up in are completely random. We can't really take credit for all our talents, although it is important to make good use of them; similarly, our flaws are not our fault, but we need to take responsibility to improve them. Being born to affluent people with access to education and healthcare does not make a person special; it makes them lucky. And being born to refugees fleeing persecution does not make a person any less important, worthy or deserving.

Non-judgment doesn't mean never making judgment calls. In compassion, we have to make judgment calls about suffering and how to help! Being non-judgmental means being willing to accept and engage with all of the complex factors that make up a person, ourselves included. And it means approaching others and ourselves in a way that is non-blaming and non-shaming. Remember, it's not our fault.

The challenge is to bring non-judgment to each moment of the day:

> I open my heart and mind to accepting everyone without judgment.
>
> When I notice myself judging, was my mind on autopilot? Can I see this person in other ways?
>
> Can I relate to this person as someone with their own triumphs and failings, as someone just like me?

Self-Reflection on Non-Judgment

Write some notes in your *Personal Practice Workbook* about how you might develop a non-judgmental approach, as well as three specific ways you could practice bringing non-judgment more into your life and relationships?

Care for Wellbeing

In nurturing compassion, we are motivated by a care for the wellbeing of all people; it is our guiding principle. This caring motivation has evolved as part of how humans survived. The greatest challenge here is to be able to let go of other motivations, especially threat-detection and avoidance, or competitiveness and self-interest.

However, if we can connect with our innate motivation and ability to care for wellbeing, then everything changes. Our awareness, thoughts, feelings and actions start to focus on identifying suffering in others or in ourselves and being motivated to help. And from care for wellbeing can emerge the courage to face difficulties and take compassionate action.

Being more compassionate means: we put thought and effort into understanding human suffering, how it arises and is maintained, and what might be most helpful in preventing or alleviating it.

Create an image in your mind of both you and someone you care about. Offer these well-wishes, quietly in your own mind:

> May you and I be safe
>
> May you and I be peaceful
>
> May you and I be healthy
>
> May you and I live with ease
>
> May you and I be free of suffering

Self-Reflection on Care for Wellbeing

Reflect for a few minutes now on what you would like to do next to develop your care for the wellbeing of others, or yourself. See if you can identify three specific actions you could take in daily life to develop your care for the wellbeing of others, or yourself. Use your *Personal Practice Workbook* to make a note of your thoughts and ideas.

Practising Compassion

His Holiness, the 14th Dalai Lama of Tibet, is widely regarded as a global authority on the importance of compassion and its impact on humanity. During an interview, he explained that there is a developmental process for cultivating compassion for others:

> The first step is knowledge …Then you need to constantly reflect and internalise this knowledge…to the point where it will become a conviction. It becomes integrated into your state of mind …Then you get to a point where it becomes spontaneous.

The Dalai Lama urges us to consider that 'merely thinking that compassion and reason and patience are good, will not be enough to develop them,' and puts forward a challenging idea:

> We must wait for difficulties to arise and then attempt to practice them. And who creates such opportunities? Not our friends, of course, but our enemies. They are the ones who give us the most trouble. So, if we truly wish to learn, we should consider enemies to be our best teacher!

For some people, this is a very radical idea. For that reason alone, it is worth giving some serious thought to it. Think of someone, perhaps a family member, friend or work colleague, with whom you are experiencing some challenges, disappointments or frustrations.

Develop a picture of that person in your mind. Feel the presence of that person. Notice the feelings that arise as you imagine this person.

Now consider and say to yourself:

> This person is just like me. Just like me, they were once a child. This person has had ups and downs. Just like me, this person has had goals and dreams. Just like me, they have strengths and qualities…they have fears and vulnerabilities…and just like me they have had successes, and they have made mistakes.

Making a Commitment

So far, we have looked at:

- compassion as a sensitivity to suffering in one's self and others and a commitment to try to alleviate and prevent it.
- the importance of striving to acquire wisdom and knowledge.
- the role of strength and groundedness.
- building the confidence and courage needed to be able to act.

Secondly, we described the attributes of a compassionate person, and explored how to:

- develop our awareness of, and sensitivity to, the suffering of ourselves and others.
- practice non-judgment and acceptance.
- nurture empathy and understanding.
- find sympathy for the hardships that we all may face.
- connect with our caring motivation to support the wellbeing of all.
- foster strength, fortitude and the ability to cope and tolerate our own distress in the presence of suffering.

Consider and reflect on your motivation for cultivating compassion. Spend a significant amount of time here, perhaps even reflecting on the following questions overnight or across the week. Take your time. This is an unfolding process, and your thoughts may change or deepen across this book. Make some initial notes in your *Personal Practice Workbook* and feel free to return to these questions throughout your compassionate journey.

> What would you LIKE to do, or change, in order to cultivate compassion?
>
> What are your personal REASONS for making these changes?
>
> What is it that makes cultivating compassion IMPORTANT to you?

> So, if you were to cultivate compassion, HOW would you go about it?

And now it's time to commit!

> What will you do next to cultivate compassion at home, at work, in your daily life, or perhaps even towards yourself?
>
> In compassion…
>
> …we become *sensitive* to the suffering of others and ourselves, with *non-judgmental acceptance* and *empathic understanding*, feeling *sympathetically moved* by this suffering and motivated by a *care for wellbeing* to offer help, while also developing our ability to *tolerate our own feelings of distress* if or when they arise.

Three Pearls

Time now to reflect on Chapter 3 and see if you can write down your three pearls about the attributes of compassion. The pearls really can be anything that comes to mind. It's just a way to pause and reflect on the ideas and practical strategies presented so far. If you like, you can use your *Personal Practice Workbook* to record your three pearls.

Chapter 4

Moving from What to How

Practicing Skills and Competencies

Having explored the six key attributes of compassion, let's now consider the skills and competencies necessary. Think of it like this — the attributes are like building blocks while the skills and competencies are the cement that holds it all together. These skills are collectively known as the second psychology of compassion; the actions we can take to cultivate compassion.

We can start to enact certain skills to give us the insight and wisdom to understand ourselves, the sources of our suffering, and what to do to alleviate or prevent it. It is very important to set an intention and make a commitment to learn, practice and eventually embody the compassionate mind.

The six skills to develop the compassionate mind are as follows:

Attention

Imagery

Reasoning

Behaviour

Sensory

Feeling

Attention

Remember when we explored the threat system? You'll recall that it's very quick to activate and it tends to narrow your attention onto possible or perceived danger. So, it's important that as we develop a compassionate mind, we practice opening up our field of attention and intentionally shifting our consideration to other, more helpful targets.

Our minds are like a spotlight, not that which it shines upon.

While we might initially place our attention on a threat we can, with practice, shift our mind's spotlight to notice what else is there, perhaps even aspects of the moment we're caught up in that could be really helpful. Or we might put our focus on remembering a useful strategy.

Consider a landlord heading off to inspect their tenanted house. The tenants have spent all day scrubbing and cleaning in preparation for the inspection, but when the landlord arrives, she immediately feels upset when she notices some pen marks on the wall. No other aspects of the clean house are noticed.

Being able to shift attention, on purpose, is invaluable. It can shift us away from rumination or worry, open us up to other options and offers us a chance to identify the next thought or action which is most useful and pragmatic.

Where we put our attention matters; it can powerfully influence how we view the world.

Imagery

The second competency, imagery, offers us the chance to capitalise on a newer function of the human brain, namely our ability to imagine.

However, we all know that the human brain has a tendency towards anxiety and is capable of creating all sorts of negative possibilities. When we imagine the worst, the effects of these images on our body are experienced as if we were facing a clear and present danger.

Alternatively, when we recall a shameful memory, even if it is from many years ago, suddenly we are feeling the inadequacy, fear and unworthiness as if it were actually happening.

The mind, and its ability to imagine, is very powerful.

However, our capacity to imagine can also be used and developed in very helpful ways.

Many meditation practitioners use guided visualisation techniques to help us calm ourselves, to feel positive emotions and to imagine we are in a safe, secure or magical place. When we bring to mind the image of a place that makes us feel peaceful, comfortable, and safe, then this too can be felt in the body, having a soothing and restorative effect.

We can use imagery to create scenarios to give us validation, reassurance, encouragement, and support. This may even involve imagery that incorporates another person as a source of compassion, such as a spiritual figure or someone who we love and admire. Eventually, we might even incorporate images of our own Compassionate Self.

Reasoning

We also work on more cognitive aspects of the mind, such as reasoning guided by wisdom, in part to ensure that our thought processes aren't creating more suffering.

We might try to challenge our own irrational thoughts if we notice ourselves thinking, for example, 'nobody likes me.' But it's important we do not do so in ways that are hostile or self-critical as that can result in us feeling worse:

'Don't be ridiculous! Of course, you have friends, you idiot.'

A calm mind thinks differently.

When it comes to reasoning, we always try to first calm down the mind and remain focused on a wise, strong, compassionate intention.

My Story

Dr Deborah Lee is a clinical psychologist in the UK and an expert on using a compassion-focused approach to the treatment of trauma. Her book is titled *The Compassionate Mind Approach to Recovering from Trauma*.

In 2018 I attended one of her workshops, and it was a particularly moving experience to hear her speak about her work, the people she works with, their experiences, and just what can help them on their journey of recovery from trauma.

When Dr Lee was talking about the skills associated with cultivating compassion, she talked about how people who have experienced trauma in childhood have experienced a violation of their most fundamental human rights. And at such a young age, this is a major blow to their sense of safeness and security, especially in relationships. The very people who should have loved them, cared for them, and protected them, have caused terror and harm. This unavoidably sows the seeds for how they feel about all their close relationships, even once they have grown up, and often throughout their lives. People, especially loved ones, are a source of threat.

The threat system is activated for people who have experienced trauma, and once activated, all they can think about is where's the next threat going to come from. They see threat everywhere, every look, comment, move from a loved one could be the beginning of the next trauma. Having described all of this, Dr Lee stood still and tall in front of her audience, took a breath, let her shoulders relax, and she said, 'But a calm mind thinks differently.'

Her comments have stuck with me ever since.

Behaviour

Compassion involves action and so cultivating the compassionate mind often means setting certain behavioural intentions and commitments. Being able to identify the actions that would be most helpful in any given situation involves drawing on the wisdom of compassion. Next, the implementation of these actions, actually doing it, takes strength and courage.

The behaviours that we might practice in order to bring compassion might include approaching when we would rather avoid, reassuring when we would rather criticise, or even doing something practical to help. Sometimes the behavioural elements of the compassionate mind might involve not taking any action and simply sitting with the situation.

May I be helpful, rather than harmful, to myself and others.

Compassionate conduct is often not the easy option and can be more uncomfortable in the short-term. Just think of starting a gym program. At first exercise can be quite unpleasant but we know that in the longer-term it is helpful and can eventually help us suffer less. We can bring a compassionate intention and motivation to help us with any given behavioural choice.

Sensory

The foundation of all these competencies is being able to pay attention to the body and to soothe, ground and calm it in different circumstances. Bringing it back to the body with posture, facial expression, voice tone and soothing rhythm breathing helps prepare us for work with compassionate imagery, reasoning and behaviour.

Always bring it back to the body.

The compassionate intention behind these competencies is also to open and deepen our awareness of ourselves and others, to learn how our minds work and how we might be able to lessen suffering.

Feeling

As a primary set of distinct feelings, we will focus in this book on anger, anxiety, and sadness. However, depending on the context, people may feel different combinations of these primary emotions, as well as many others besides.

Feelings tend to be spontaneous.

Developing competencies around the awareness and understanding of emotions does not mean that we are expecting to directly stimulate or manipulate the feelings themselves. Nor does strengthening a compassionate mind mean that we can immediately reduce anxiety or anger as if taking a medication. Rather, as we deepen our understanding and acceptance of difficult emotions, we are more and more able to let go of them. After all, when we struggle with the way we feel, we ultimately suffer more. On the other hand, we can find ways to connect other feeling states, such as feelings of warmth, safeness, groundedness and confidence. All of these competencies can be brought to the task of softening difficult emotions, and connecting with positive emotions.

Three Pearls

Chapter 4 really started to explore how to cultivate compassion, the skills and competencies associated with compassion. Perhaps there are three pearls you could record in your *Personal Practice Workbook*, to remember, reflect upon, or put into practice.

Chapter 5

Mindfulness and Imagery, Attention and Safeness

Attention Training with Mindfulness

Mindfulness is part of ancient wisdom and spiritual traditions, and its rich complexity will not be explored in detail here. Having said that, mindfulness can also be described more simply as different layers of present moment awareness; but to achieve it takes some practice.

One popular definition by meditation pioneer Jon Kabat-Zinn is that mindfulness is 'bringing our attention, nonjudgmentally, and purposefully, to the present moment.'

Being mindful means being consciously aware of our thoughts, feelings, body sensations and behaviours *as they arise*. It can also include awakening our senses in the present moment and observing what we can see, hear, touch, smell, and taste.

For our purpose, mindfulness is a pathway to compassion. It helps us to step out of autopilot and into a state of present moment awareness and nonjudgmental attention. This allows and encourages us to connect with our wisdom. We can then make choices about how we want to respond, rather than being reactive. This is especially true of bringing our conscious mind to moments of suffering.

The majority of us spend more time than we realise on autopilot, lost in our own thoughts. This means that whatever comes to mind gets automatically translated into feelings, urges, and ultimately reactive behaviours.

This is a moment of suffering.
What can I do next that would be most helpful?

It's not easy. The busy human brain naturally seeks constant distraction, and it's very tempting to think 'Oh, I am not good at being mindful. My thoughts are all over the place.'

You're not alone. Remember that everyone's brain has a tendency to do this. So be gentle with yourself and quietly bring your attention back to the task at hand. There is no right or wrong way to practice mindfulness and to connect to your inner stillness. Rather it is a process of remembering to be aware of the present moment, noticing when that awareness drifts away, and remembering to return to the practice.

Ngaire

>For a long time Ngaire said she had been so depressed that she was unable to find the motivation to leave the house. There were days when she could barely walk down to her front gate to collect her mail. Most of her friends had drifted away, her family always seemed angry at her, and she was altogether socially disconnected and alone. She felt immobilised by her painful thoughts and feelings, constantly ruminating over her life and losses, mistakes and failures, and felt hopeless about herself and her future.

>I was well aware of just how stuck she was, and we were finding any improvement difficult to achieve. Then one day she shocked me. She casually mentioned that she had been to her skydiving lesson at that previous weekend! Skydiving? 'Yes,' she said as if this were nothing significant at all. When I recovered from the shock, and we had a playful chuckle at how much she had surprised me, Ngaire went on to reveal that this was something that she did on a regular basis. In fact, she said she had skydiving lessons on an almost monthly basis but had not thought it important enough to mention.

I was absolutely stunned. This woman was amazing! Despite the severity of her depression, she was managing to get to skydiving lessons. So we explored this behaviour in detail, trying to understand how all this might make sense for her. Eventually, as if it was an afterthought, Ngaire described how, when she was skydiving, all her difficult thoughts and feelings, all her ruminating, seemed to fade into the background. 'It's like I become one with that moment in time,' she said, 'And I get a break from all that negative chatter in my head.' Quite by accident, Ngaire had discovered mindfulness.

Many people are drawn to activities where they can be mindful. They don't necessarily realise that's what they're doing; but think about pastimes such as fishing, reading, playing music, drawing or painting, and sport. Some people love going to work because they can bring mindful attention to the task at hand, and let go of other thoughts and feelings. I've always enjoyed cycling. When I'm on a busy road peddling along, I simply have to be aware of my surroundings. This is how I let go of the troubles and strife of the day, and practise mindfulness.

The challenge is to be able to be mindful in moments when there isn't much going on, nothing to grab the attention. With the memory and feelings of skydiving in mind, Ngaire started to develop and practice that skill when she was home, alone, and feeling stuck with her thoughts.

I always admired the progress she made from there, and the lessons she taught me along the way.

Mindfulness of Thoughts

Try a mindfulness practice now. Firstly, sit comfortably in your chair, with your feet flat on the floor, arms and legs uncrossed, and your hands resting in your lap.

Allow yourself to settle into the present moment.

Bring your awareness to your body, especially to the sensations of touch or pressure where your body makes contact with the chair or floor. Mentally scan your entire body from top to bottom, noticing any tension or uneasiness and, as best you can, try and let those sensations soften.

And now, slowly bring your awareness to the gentle rising and falling of your breath in your chest or belly. Like ocean waves coming in and going out, your breath is always there. Notice its rhythm in your body, the inhale and the exhale, and the sensations in your chest and belly as you breathe in, and as you breathe out.

Notice the cool and fresh air as it flows in through your nostrils, then passes through your airways, filling your lungs. Your chest rises and then falls as the air swirls out of your lungs again, out through your nostrils just that little bit warmer. Take a few moments to simply notice the sensations as you breathe in and out.

Say to yourself: 'I notice I am breathing in; I notice I am breathing out.' There is no need to try to control your breathing. Simply allow and accept it as it is.

Sooner or later, your focus will wander away from the breath to other thoughts, worries, images, bodily sensations, plans, or daydreams. That's perfectly okay. Just start to notice the thoughts as they come. The thinking mind is part of experience. There's no reason to try to stop the thoughts or exclude the thinking mind from your practice. Just notice the thoughts as they come, with curiosity.

Observing thoughts is a bit like seeing a stranger walking past your front fence. You may notice the person; you may even nod your head or give them a wave of acknowledgement. But you don't need to invite them in. You can just let them pass by. So, it is with mindfulness — you can notice thoughts, acknowledge them, and then let them pass by.

Simply notice the thought coming up into your awareness and notice when it goes. You may use one-word labels to notice the thoughts 'planning', 'worrying', 'analysing', 'regretting'. Or perhaps simply 'thinking of the past' or 'thinking of the future'. Don't attach to the thoughts or push them away, but bring mindfulness to them, noticing them with detachment, noticing them come and go.

When you are ready, take a few final mindful breaths, noticing how you feel. And then, gently wriggle your fingers and toes and gradually bring a little movement to the whole body. When you're ready, you can bring this practice gently to a close.

Safety Versus Safeness

Safety is a way of being that arises from the threat system as a means of seeking protection. When we are in safety mode, our attention is focused, our imagination conjures up all of the possible threats, and our conduct is directed toward dealing with possible danger while preventing bad things from happening.

Safety mode makes a lot of sense from an evolutionary point of view. Imagine the prehistoric humans making their way along the forest path. They weren't looking around gazing at the pretty butterflies as they flew through the dancing sunbeams that shone through gaps among the leaves of the canopy high above. They were much more likely too busy furtively scanning their surroundings and thinking to themselves, 'Where's the bear?' And rightly so!

For modern humans, being in safety mode might involve avoiding certain people, places or scenarios; simply staying home can feel like the safest thing sometimes to avoid disapproval or social rejection. For people who have trauma histories, being in safety mode can understandably become quite prominent as a method of coping.

If the trauma was specific, such as a car accident, then safety mode may be at its peak of activation around traffic. However, when the trauma was experienced in a much more pervasive way, over long periods or involving significant caregivers, then the activation of safety mode can be quite prevalent, or even constant.

Safeness, however, is associated with the soothing system; with a sense of safeness, we can relax, settle into the moment, and be playful where we are and with what we're doing. Experiencing safeness, we have the freedom to explore, expand our horizons, and try out new things.

Think of the toddler who feels safe with her Dad. They have a little cuddle and when she looks up at him, he smiles and says in a gentle, friendly tone, 'Go on.' She climbs off his lap, gets to her feet and then happily wanders towards the play equipment. This can be what safeness is like: a sense of assurance and security to explore the world.

Both safety and safeness are important; when crossing the road it's important to be in safety mode to keep yourself free from harm, and once you have safely crossed to the other side you can once again experience a sense of safeness.

Our goal is to access both safety and safeness, and our primary challenge is to bring mindfulness and attention to our moment-to-moment experience of them. We also want to be able to develop our skill in shifting between both states; wisdom and courage are important in terms of knowing when safety mode might no longer be necessary and the shift to safeness is appropriate and vice versa.

Safe Place Imagery

To bring about a sense of safeness in the mind and the body we use imagery to activate our soothing system.

It's important to acknowledge that most of us find it hard to create vivid and lasting images in our minds. Images are commonly experienced as fleeting impressions, a momentary sense of a place or time. The brain is very powerful, and images in our minds can quickly translate to sensations in our bodies even when the image is only short-lived. This is true for all images, whether they prompt anxious feelings or happy ones.

Start by preparing your body as we did before. Find your compassionate posture, with your shoulders back and chest open, hands relaxed in your lap, and a friendly expression on your face. Bring your attention to your breath and find the soothing rhythm that works best for you, perhaps breathing in for a count of five, and out for a count of five.

Begin by bringing to mind an image of a place where you feel comfortable, peaceful, and safe. Perhaps it's a peaceful beach scene, a mountain view, a park or even your own backyard. Inside or out, night or day, warm or cool, begin to bring this image to life by noticing details. Look around and observe the features or objects that may be present such as trees, grass, or rocks. Breathe in the air or scent and notice any sounds or sensations of touch or smell.

This safe place is somewhere you truly belong. It's like the features or objects of this place are happy to see you and welcome you there. They smile and say with a friendly voice, 'Hello! Welcome.'

You are absolutely safe to explore this place. Would you like to move about or just relax? Be creative with the possibilities of what to do next.

The only guideline is that you enjoy being in your safe place, doing whatever makes you feel emotionally secure and relaxed.

When you're ready, let the image of your safe place begin to fade. Bring a little movement back to your body, wriggling fingers and toes, and gradually come back to the present moment.

Matteo

Sometimes people can imagine the most unexpected safe places!

Matteo was a young man in his twenties who came along to work out his concerns with social anxiety. He was terribly affected by social anxiety, and despite being a smart, interesting, adventurous guy, he really panicked when it came to meeting new people, or worse, meeting people for a second time (he said the expectations felt even higher then and he was even more likely to disappoint people).

Social anxiety had caused him to avoid going to university lectures, speaking with his professors, or taking part in group assignments, which ultimately meant he withdrew from his engineering studies. He was working full time when I met him, but it was torturous given he was now working at a grocery store and kept being promoted! He thought he could just pack shelves, but managers would quickly see his talents and give him more responsibilities, promoting him up the chain. When I met him, he was the fruit and vegetable supervisor.

At work, and anytime he was out and about really, he was in safety mode, always looking for social threat and danger, and ready to respond defensively. He persisted with work because he needed to support himself, but much of the rest of the time he stayed home. So at one point in therapy we tried to work with some safe place imagery. I didn't expect the image he came up with!

Matteo described how he had imagined himself rock climbing. In his imagery, he was perched high up on a cliff face, fingers and toes gripping the nooks and crannies of the rock, searching for his next handhold. He said that the exercise made him feel safe and free. I mentioned that it sounded almost scary to me, and he said, 'Well, once I've done my safety check, I know my ropes are secure, and I feel confident about all that, then I am right to go, and I feel completely safe.'

This was real wisdom from Matteo, and we worked with this a lot over the coming sessions. Of course, he recognised that the other aspect of this image was the absence of any other people. So we gradually introduced another person into the image, someone he felt he could trust and feel safe with, someone who could be down on the ground 'on belay'. And gradually we were able to introduce other elements of affiliation, cooperation and support from other people to the image, all of which became something of a metaphor for his real life, and introduced a sense of safeness elsewhere in his day-to-day.

Imagery is really a very powerful skill. We will be using imagery like this throughout the book in various ways. In the next chapter we will be creating images of an ideal compassionate other and our ideal Compassionate Self. These images will then be brought to more difficult thoughts and feelings, and helping to work with our own suffering, as we make our way through subsequent chapters.

Three Pearls

Chapter 5 explored mindfulness and imagery, especially safe place imagery. This will come up again and again as we proceed through the book. Take note in your *Personal Practice Workbook* of three pearls to remember, reflect upon, or put into practice.

Chapter 6

Compassionate Other, Compassionate Self

Using Imagery to Create an Ideal Compassionate Being

We begin this process by bringing to mind a compassionate person or another living being from your life. This might be a parent, grandparent, family member, friend, teacher, fictional character or even a beloved pet. Some people even choose objects from nature such as rivers, trees or mountains and imbue them with human qualities.

Examples might include a grandmother who was full of warmth and cuddles, a golden dragon who was wise and protective, a superhero who was strong and brave, or a beloved dog from one's childhood who possessed all of these characteristics.

For the purposes of creating the image of an 'ideal compassionate other', we might draw on people we've known and then create an ideal being that is wise, strong, courageous, committed, and helpful. This ideal compassionate other does not suffer from the usual human weaknesses or flaws, but rather is exactly who you would want them to be.

Whatever form you choose, this ideal compassionate being understands the human condition and is compassionate towards your struggles.

In order to bring this being to life in your imagination perhaps you can consider:

- How would you like your ideal compassionate other to appear?
- What gender would you like them to be?
- What is their age?
- How would you describe their shape, size, or stature?
- What sort of facial expressions would your ideal compassionate other have?
- How might they communicate with you, such as their tone of voice?

Now start to consider the kind of personal qualities or characteristics that you would like your ideal compassionate other to have. While you might imagine qualities such as wisdom, strength, courage, and commitment a range of other qualities can also be included such as patience, tolerance, friendliness, gentleness, and humour. There are many possible aspects to the ideal compassionate other, so give yourself time to create the image of a being that has all the qualities you're comfortable with, or that you would really like them to have.

Going Deeper with the Ideal Compassionate Other

Now you have a sense of the appearance of your ideal compassionate other, let's flesh out the qualities of wisdom, strength and courage, and commitment to be friendly, supportive, helpful and caring.

Remember that, however your ideal compassionate other may appear, they have a mind that understands the human brain, how it evolved, the way that it is tricky and gets caught in loops, and that it can be the source of suffering for ourselves and others. This is a great source of wisdom, knowing and understanding that suffering is a part of life and not your fault.

Create a more detailed image of your ideal compassionate other. For example, what is their backstory? How did they obtain this wisdom and understanding? How might they express or convey their wisdom in a way that might help you to feel safe and soothed? Remember that they understand human thoughts, feelings, and behaviours and do not judge.

The qualities of strength and courage in your ideal compassionate other are infused with friendliness and helpfulness. They do not want to control you or tell you what to do; conversely, they are not passive, submissive or weak. The key is that they have a sense of emotional strength, solidness, and stableness. Through their own expression of strength and courage, they are able to inspire us to feel encouraged, confident and assertive.

When you think of the emotional strength and courage that the ideal compassionate other possesses how might that be evident or expressed in them? What sorts of skills or abilities might they have that helps them to be supportive and helpful, or even protective? Imagine too how they might bring their emotional strength and courage to being able to tolerate your distress, pain and suffering?

Finally, we want to elaborate on the commitment of our ideal compassionate other to understand you and your mind, and to help you become more soothed, settled and balanced. They have a commitment to help you to be sensitive to your own suffering and committed to alleviating and preventing that suffering. They want you to build a life in which you can thrive and flourish.

Relating to the Ideal Compassionate Other

Having created a sense of our ideal compassionate other, we now start to practice imagining how we might relate to this being and how this being might in turn relate to us. At this stage, approach this exercise in an open-hearted and playful way.

We begin, as always, by bringing our attention to the body and creating our compassionate posture: sitting comfortably, feet flat on the floor, shoulders back and hands resting gently on your lap. Bring your attention and awareness to your face and create a friendly expression.

And when you are ready, begin the practice of soothing rhythm breathing, gradually slowing down your mind and body.

We always try to respect the practice by first preparing the body. This is not unlike warming up the body prior to physical activity. We create a compassionate bodily state with posture, facial expression, tone of voice, and soothing rhythm breathing.

This exercise will use imagery to help us relate to our ideal compassionate other. We will be working with the image of a being who is fully committed to understanding, supporting, and encouraging us. Notice what happens in your mind and your body as we go through this exercise, so remain aware of any changes in the mind and body.

Bring to mind a minor life challenge that you are currently struggling with, something that has brought you disappointment, or some anxiety or frustration. Spend a few moments just reflecting on it.

Next, imagine you're with your ideal compassionate other, perhaps seated across from one another or side-by-side, however you feel most comfortable. Spend a few moments bringing to mind the image of this being with their wisdom, strength and courage, and commitment to your wellbeing. Add any other qualities that you might want from a compassionate other, such as patience, humour, or kindness.

How do you want your ideal compassionate other to relate you regarding this life difficulty or challenge? What would be the emotional quality of their general presence? What do you imagine would be the quality of their voice tone? What might they say or do to help you feel heard and understood, and to connect you to wisdom?

How do you imagine you might relate to this ideal compassionate other? What kinds of things would you like to say or do? What would you like to express or share? Remember you can say or do anything you like, and this ideal compassionate other will deeply understand you and stay committed to being helpful.

One of the purposes of imagining an ideal compassionate other and having a conversation about any particular life difficulty or challenge is to help us. Remember that a calm mind thinks differently, so this practical use of imagery can help us from getting lost in unhelpful thoughts and feelings. Instead it allows us to step back, take different perspectives, and find ways to alleviate suffering, or prevent further or worse distress.

My Story

> When I first participated in this practice, the ideal compassionate other who came to mind was my old dog Hammer. He was already gone at the time I first tried this, however, his image sprang to mind immediately, symbolising those important attributes.
>
> Hammer was a Saint Bernard, German Shepherd cross, 55 kilograms of loveliness. He would stand on his back legs and put his front paws on my shoulders, and we would stand there, gazing into each others' eyes (until his breath would eventually overwhelm me!).
>
> One night, when all was shrouded in darkness and silence, I remember Hammer's single, yet insistent, 'woof!' It roused me a little, and then there was another single, yet insistent, 'woof!' 'Hammer!' I yelled back. There was a pause, and then another single, yet insistent, 'woof!' I thought it strange, and different, and so I dragged myself out of bed to investigate.
>
> A glow started to appear as I rounded the corner and, to my horror, a grass fire in the vacant block next door was erupting, unknown cause, getting perilously close to the edge of the house in which we were sleeping. I raced outside and began dousing it with the garden hose. Hammer had saved us!
>
> It gives me shivers, and emotion pushes out behind my eyes when I think about it. Even now, more than 20 years later.
>
> So, in that first time I created my ideal compassionate other, Hammer was the compassionate friend that immediately appeared. His face was cheerful, friendly, with attentive eyes. He felt warm, brave and full of love. And he said to me, 'You are ok, you belong.' And then he gave me a ball. He loved chasing balls. But then the ball turned into the world and suddenly, there I was, with the whole world in my hands.
>
> A very powerful practice indeed.

Describing Your Ideal Compassionate Other

It is important to spend some time creatively describing your *ideal* compassionate other. Remember, this compassionate other is ideal, and so doesn't have the faults and flaws of the rest of us. This compassionate other is just right.

You will find space in your *Personal Practice Workbook* to write down your answers to several guiding questions to help with describing your ideal compassionate other, including the following:

- How would you like you ideal compassionate other to look?
- How would you like your ideal compassionate other to sound?
- How would you like your ideal compassionate other to feel?
- How would you like your ideal compassionate other to relate to you?
- How would you like to relate to your ideal compassionate other?
- How would you like your ideal compassionate other to be in terms of:
  - Wisdom?
  - Strength and courage?
  - Commitment?

Compassion as a Brain Pattern

We have talked about the attributes and skills of a compassionate person and started to use imagery to develop a felt sense of an ideal compassionate other. This has been designed as a way to facilitate the opening up of our ability to receive compassion from others. Next, we will explore how to cultivate those same attributes, skills, and qualities of compassion in ourselves and for ourselves.

To begin this explanation, we start by considering compassion as being a particular version of ourselves. We have many versions of ourselves; we have the self who goes to a job interview, the self who is pulled over by a police officer, the self who wants a particular romantic outcome. Some of these different versions we might choose to enact, however, some simply turn up automatically. One particular version that we will focus on now can be thought of as the 'Compassionate Self.'

The Compassionate Self involves choosing a version of ourselves that is wise, strong, courageous, and committed to our own wellbeing. We can start to actively choose to become this version of ourselves in any given moment rather than falling into other less helpful automatic portrayals.

Just like an accountant, carpenter, or teacher turns up to work every day choosing to play their professional role, so we too can choose the role of the Compassionate Self. The Compassionate Self is a version of ourselves that is coming from a caring motivation, activating the old brain and body systems that allow us to function in caring ways, and then using new functions to practice and enact ways of being helpful, rather than harmful, to ourselves and others.

We often believe that, at our core, we have one true and authentic self, but in reality there are many different versions of who we are, depending on the context. We have lots of different brain patterns and resulting systems of behaviour, but the good news is that we can step out of an automatic reactive state into a more intentional mode of being. Through practice we can eventually embody this more compassionate version of ourselves and this self can then become the strongest! And so, we cultivate wisdom, strength and courage, empathy, and a genuine desire and commitment to be helpful to ourselves and others.

Compassion for Others

One really useful way to explore the Compassionate Self is to recall an experience where you were compassionate towards somebody else who was struggling or suffering.

Compassion flows in three directions, and for many people offering compassion to others is the most comfortable and relatable direction. Exploring a time when we have shown compassion towards somebody else can be a great way to access the attention, thoughts, feelings, and sensations of the body, of your Compassionate Self.

If you can, bring to mind a memory of a time where you wanted to help somebody who was suffering. The focus need not be on the other person's suffering itself or what has caused it, but rather on your wish to be helpful and how that changed the observable patterns of the brain and body. What did you notice you were paying attention to? What sorts of thoughts were you having? And what sensations did you feel in your body? You may recall feeling alert or even on edge. This is perfectly normal and speaks to the importance of distress tolerance.

Further, what was it that you wanted to do so as to be helpful? Notice that a part of you possessed the intuitive wisdom of how to be helpful. It's so interesting to see how a compassionate motivation arises quite automatically, even though the action component can look different depending on the situation and the people involved.

And this is the key. Compassion is a motivation, and when it's activated it can result in changes to our whole system; it can become a very powerful way of dealing with difficulties when we learn more about it, practice it, and embody it. In the same way we can learn to drive, practice for a number of hours and eventually it becomes second nature. Cultivating our Compassionate Self is very similar.

Lights, Camera, Action!

Actors use several techniques to convincingly play their roles. One of them is method acting which involves adopting the physical and psychological attributes of the character they are playing.

Imagine you are an actor. The stage director asks you to walk down an alley (which has been constructed on the set) and when a thug jumps out from behind a wall you have to depict fear and panic. How would you do it? Perhaps you could put this book down right now and try it. You could probably also act out the angry thug or even the police officer who comes to the rescue.

We have the capability to shift across different body states and states of mind through the process of acting; our ability to do this provides an exquisite opportunity to use method acting to shift into the Compassionate Self.

We have already discussed the qualities that you would like in your ideal compassionate other, now consider what you would like to have as compassionate qualities for yourself. Record your thoughts about the key qualities that you would truly love to have if you could be at your compassionate best in your *Personal Practice Workbook*.

People often generate lists of qualities that include many of the key attributes of compassion: empathy, acceptance, patience, tolerance, friendliness, helpfulness, and so on. Note how these qualities emerge from your intuitive wisdom around compassion.

A quick reminder that when developing compassion, we always try to include the qualities of *wisdom*, *strength* and *courage*, and *commitment.*

We tap into our wisdom and understanding about the human brain and that we are shaped by life experiences, which none of us gets to choose, and which at times can cause chaos and suffering. And this is not our fault! And we can tap into the wisdom of how to cope with the difficulties we might face, and how to help others in the face of their difficulties.

We tap into our strength and courage, fortitude and authority by using the body and breath to ground ourselves and establish stability, confidence and poise.

We might also explore our own values with respect to how we believe we should treat ourselves and others and use those values to strengthen our commitment to be helpful rather than harmful, as well as promoting wellbeing.

If you have decided to develop these qualities so that you were more patient, friendly, or helpful, how would you go about that on a day-to-day basis or over the next week or month? Remember that while we want to eventually embody these qualities, we can only do so step by step over a period of time; this type of deep change cannot be achieved at all once. We start by intentionally enacting our own 'Compassionate Self'.

Beginning to Imagine Your Compassionate Self

Please assume a comfortable position, upright and reasonably relaxed, and take a few moments now to find a soothing rhythm to your breathing.

We will start to imagine what you would feel, think and experience if you were a deeply compassionate person who had already succeeded in developing these qualities.

You might bring to mind a compassionate person who has these qualities and imagine how it might feel to be like that person.

Imagine that your body feels safe, peaceful and comfortable. Imagine that your body is flowing with *warmth*. Perhaps bring a gentle, friendly smile to your face. Imagine that alongside these feelings of safeness and warmth, you embody a committed motivation to help those who are suffering, others, and also yourself. Imagine that this *caring commitment* grows within you, filling you with a sense of purpose; a deep desire to be helpful.

May I be helpful, rather than harmful, to myself and others.

Imagine that this caring commitment is aided by *wisdom*. You understand the nature of the human brain, and that it was designed for us, over millions of years of evolution, and not designed by us. And while it is powerful and has helped us survive, it comes along with trade-offs and can be a source of great suffering.

Certain difficult feelings, thoughts and sensations, urges and desires, and certain actions arise from our tricky brains that we would really rather not have. This is not our fault. And yet part of your wisdom is knowing that our brains can also learn, change and grow, and we can gradually take responsibility for our minds, bringing awareness and intention our lives.

It's not my fault, but it is my responsibility.

You are able to bring mindfulness and mind awareness to difficult situations, knowing that they too will pass. And so, with non-judgment and acceptance of yourself and others, you understand the origins of these feelings, thoughts, physical sensations and behaviours, and how all of this makes complete sense.

Imagine that with this caring commitment and wisdom, you possess immense *strength* and *courage*. You can cultivate a sense of calmness, groundedness and stability, and the determination to engage with difficulties, with the confidence that you can cope and be helpful. Use the body and the breath to connect with those feelings of strength, groundedness and stability.

A calm mind thinks differently.

Imagine that you already possess these qualities — a caring commitment to be helpful, innate and growing wisdom and understanding of human suffering, and inner strength, groundedness and stability, as well as emotional courage, to approach suffering, in yourself and others, and do something to try to help.

How does it feel to bring awareness to these qualities building within you? How would you feel as this Compassionate Self? What would you look like, your posture, facial expression and the way you would move? How might you approach the world and the people or other living beings that you come across as your Compassionate Self? What would you understand? What emotions would you feel? What kind of thoughts would you think? What would you feel motivated to do? What would you do?

Take a moment to explore and savour your Compassionate Self, and then see if you can proceed to the next section of this book, or into the rest of your day, maintaining this sense of caring commitment, wisdom, strength and courage, and compassion.

Walking About as Your Compassionate Self

This is where the idea of method acting really comes into play! Take an opportunity to stand up, assume a compassionate posture and friendly facial expression, take a few slow and soothing breaths, and walk around as if you are a wise, strong and courageous, and committed compassionate person.

You can take this practice anywhere, down the street, at work or at home. Really see if you can hold that feeling in your body; even take short breaks across the day to reconnect with your Compassionate Self when you need to. Focus on a desire to be helpful to anyone you meet. Try and convey friendliness irrespective of how you might actually be feeling. And send good wishes to people whom you may pass or meet, or people that simply come to mind.

As you practice your Compassionate Self through these method-acting techniques watch out for some of the fears, blocks and resistances we mentioned earlier. Sometimes when people act out the Compassionate Self, they worry that they might present a version of themselves that is very soft, pitying or even weak. This is why we often emphasise wisdom and strength, to really clarify what compassion is all about.

Sometimes people act out the Compassionate Self in order to create a wonderful or blissful state of mind and body. But compassion does not involve an expectation to *ascend* into a satisfying state, but is about having the courage to *descend* into disappointment, challenge, struggle and suffering, and remain present and aware. Compassion asks us to become involved with the hardest aspects of life and be willing to get our hands dirty!

Once you have practiced your Compassionate Self, you may wish to focus on someone you care about by sending them a wish to be free of suffering. Then you can bring into focus someone you don't like or someone who has caused you distress and send them the same wishes. You don't need to like them or want to see them; having compassion is not the same as liking or loving. Sometimes our greatest opportunities to practice and hone our compassion are with those who have caused us pain.

May you be free from suffering.

Notice how sending these well-wishes feels in your body and mind; there is no right way to experience these practices, rather it is a process of exploration and discovery. All these practices can be approached with a sense of gentle curiosity and playfulness. Certainly, if you practice more hostile wishes of maleficence for another person then you will feel quite different!

Using the Compassionate Self with a Life Difficulty

A core premise of this approach is that when we imagine ourselves as our Compassionate Self, and start to think and feel, move and act as if we were that person, then we can experience our problems differently. We can see things from different or new perspectives, and start to come up with alternative ways of managing our problems.

Having created a Compassionate Self, we begin to become more skilful at activating it whenever we want to. Remember: respect the practice, prepare the body. Follow the now-familiar steps of grounding your body, assuming a compassionate posture, creating a friendly facial expression and inner tone of voice, and slowing your breath. Finally, connect with the three core qualities, wisdom, strength and courage, and make a commitment to wellbeing.

Now, see if you can bring to mind a difficult situation (nothing too major at this stage) that you are currently experiencing. As you think about this, consider what your upset self is thinking, wanting, and feeling. Consider too what your upset self might do in response to this difficult situation.

Now start to consider this difficult situation from your Compassionate Self's perspective. How would you ideally like to think about this difficult situation, if you were at your wisest, strongest, most committed compassionate best? What is it that your Compassionate Self wants for you in this situation? Having considered things from the perspective of the Compassionate Self, how does this leave you feeling now? Consider how you might respond and write your thoughts in your *Personal Practice Workbook*.

Julie

>Julie was a young woman studying at university and living on campus at one of the university colleges. We had started to imagine her Compassionate Self, and work with a difficult life situation in which two other young women from college had invited a few people out for dinner on a Friday night but she hadn't been invited.
>
>What is your Upset Self thinking?
>
>*I was thinking how no one there seems to like me, I'm just not fitting in. And I might never make any friends.*
>
>What is your Compassionate Self thinking?
>
>*Well, first of all, I thought that this isn't easy. Being away from home, in a strange place, trying to meet people. And then I thought it'll probably be ok, I just need to find my people. I'm sure they are out there!*
>
>What is your Upset Self wanting?
>
>*I just desperately want to be included.*
>
>What is your Compassionate Self wanting?

My Compassionate Self just wants me to be ok, to bide my time. Not give up! But just to feel more calm about it all and see what happens.

What is your Upset Self feeling?

I was feeling hurt and lonely, but also angry...why couldn't they just include me?

What is your Compassionate Self feeling?

When I was imagining my Compassionate Self, it was like I was feeling a little sad. Maybe it was sympathy? But I was also feeling kind of gutsy, if that makes sense?

What might you do as your Upset Self?

Well, I really wanted to lash out, if I'm honest. I felt like going down the hall to their rooms and breaking something.

What might you do as your Compassionate Self?

Well, I'd do the breathing exercises first of all! And then I think I would just focus on some others I have connected a bit with, not so much at college, but through my course. Maybe even see if they are interested in meeting outside of classes.

Three Pearls

Now we are really getting somewhere in Chapter 6 with cultivating compassion, and especially the Compassionate Self. Record three pearls about your compassionate other and Compassionate Self in your *Personal Practice Workbook*.

Chapter 7

We are Made Up of Many Different Parts

Multiplicity, and Working with Multiple Selves

We are composed of several versions of ourselves, and these different forms relate to particular patterns of the brain and body. There really isn't any single 'me', but rather multiple versions depending on different contexts.

When we talk about multiple selves, we are referring to activation across a number of domains: thoughts, feelings, bodily sensations, behavioural tendencies, and specific memories and motives associated with that state. There is a desire within the pattern of our multiple selves to settle our emotions — whether that be in helpful or unhelpful ways. What we are trying to do as we cultivate our compassionate minds is bring clarity and calm to our own multiplicity and the patterns of activation that relate to each of the multiple selves.

We start to discover the forms our multiple selves can take, including anger, anxiety, sadness, and so on. Each of these selves can want different things, think in varied ways, have contrasting urges, desires, and motives — sometimes all at the same time! So, we need to identify and differentiate our multiple selves and reintegrate them via the Compassionate Self. By doing so, we can transform old emotional patterns and reduce suffering.

Anger, anxiety and sadness emerge largely from our threat system. Anger is often linked to a sense of transgression, obstruction, or violation. Anxiety is most associated with threat, danger, and vulnerability. Sadness is related to loss. These three emotions are the ones most closely allied with mental health difficulties. While there are other prominent emotions such as jealousy, envy, disgust, and shame, when we scratch the surface, we usually find that anger, anxiety and sadness are common across all of them.

Let's look at each of these main threat-based patterns of the self. In order to do so, bring to mind a recent difficult interpersonal situation, perhaps with a person you care about. It may be a recent altercation or argument which gave rise to a range of strong emotions. Keep this situation in mind as we start to differentiate these three threat-based patterns, *anger*, *anxiety*, and *sadness*, as they may have been present in your response to this situation.

You will be able to record your thoughts in the space provided in your *Personal Practice Workbook*.

Angry Self

Often in an altercation or argument, anger is the most prominent, activating emotion which drives us towards action. So, let's explore this situation from the point of view of your Angry Self. We will be considering what was said, how it was said, what you were thinking, feeling, and wanting to do or say.

As we do so, it's helpful to consider each of our multiple selves from the point of view of *motives*. By motives, we are really referring to the wants and wishes behind the multiple selves. In the case of anger, there are a number of questions to help us reflect on the motives of the Angry Self.

What was the trigger for your anger, and what did your Angry Self want in this situation? From the Angry Self's point of view, what would have been a good outcome? What was the function or purpose of Angry Self? Was there a risk of harm that Angry Self was motivated to prevent?

What was the anger trying to defend you against or protect you from? And finally, what were you worried might happen if you did not have your Angry Self? Other motives can be seeking justice, retribution, or vengeance. Were any of these playing a role in your Angry Self? You might like to record your thoughts in the space provided in your *Personal Practice Workbook*.

Understanding the motives of Angry Self really starts to clarify its function. It can also be useful to consider the *thoughts* of your Angry Self. What was your Angry Self actually thinking? What was going through your Angry Self's mind? What thoughts arose in your mind in this difficult interpersonal situation when Angry Self became present?

And what about the *bodily sensations* that went along with Angry Self? The body often reacts very automatically, but this can go unnoticed in the moment. It can therefore be very useful to reflect on what happened in your body when Angry Self was present. What were you feeling in your body, and where were you feeling it? What did you notice about your body's posture? What about the way your facial expression changed when Angry Self was present? You might like to record your thoughts in the space provided in your *Personal Practice Workbook*.

We're building an awareness of the patterns that emerge when we are in the mode of Angry Self. This awareness is very important in developing empathy, understanding the perspective and the felt experience of ourselves or others, and in the context of sympathy, or feeling moved by the experience.

Next, we want to explore the behavioural urges and *actions* of the Angry Self. In that situation, what did Angry Self want to do? If it was free to do anything it liked, what would the Angry Self have done? Sometimes we might have certain fantasies that we would never enact, but it is important to understand those urges in order to understand the patterns associated with Angry Self. Aggression, verbally and physically, storming out or abrupt withdrawal, passive aggression, stonewalling, and disengaging are all examples of behavioural urges or actions associated with Angry Self.

It is also very important to reflect upon earlier experiences and how associated *memories* may also be present for the Angry Self. When

Angry Self is present, what sorts of memories come to mind? What memories of other conflict or hurt that you associate with feeling angry are playing a role in the pattern of your Angry Self? And how far back do those memories go?

Finally, we reflect upon what strategies help to *settle* or regulate the Angry Self. How do you cope with anger? What works best at helping Angry Self to settle? Sometimes people might settle themselves by leaving the situation and going for a walk, while others might try to calm down by getting drunk and having a fight with someone else. Some of these strategies could be very helpful, but clearly, others just make matters worse.

Here's a worked example of the Angry Self:

Motives	I just wish they would listen to me and stop speaking over me. I want to teach them a lesson.
Thoughts	How dare you treat me this way. You are selfish and rude, and you think I am stupid.
Body	I get really red in the face and I start to cry. I cry when I am angry. And I feel so tense in the arms and shoulders. I can't breathe.
Actions	I yell, and I throw my hands in the air and shake my fists. I tell them it's all their fault.
Memories	This situation reminds me of times when I was a child and my brother was dismissive. He would ignore me and not listen.
Settle	Sometimes I just sob and eventually settle down. And yelling gets it off my chest. But usually I just hide away and cry.

Anxious Self

In any given situation, there are often multiple selves activated at the same time. Even when the situation is an altercation or argument, rarely are we purely in the mode of Angry Self. Quite possibly there is also activation of the Anxious Self, another threat-based emotion. As mentioned above, anxiety is often a response to threat, danger or vulnerability.

Using the situation you just examined with respect to anger, go through the same process with a focus on the part of you that was in the mode of Anxious Self. Just focus on that sense of concern, worry, or fear that you felt and let the anger aspect of it fade into the background. Bring your attention solely to the Anxious Self.

Once again, we want to try and identify the *motives* of the Anxious Self. What is the Anxious Self really concerned with? What threat or danger is it trying to protect you from? What is the Anxious Self defending you against? What does the Anxious Self see as its purpose in this situation? What do you think might happen if the Anxious Self was not around?

And then explore the Anxious Self's *thoughts*. What are the mental patterns of your Anxious Self? What thoughts are actually coming to mind in this situation?

What are the *bodily sensations* associated with the Anxious Self? What happens to your breathing and internal state? What happens externally and to the extremities? What happens to the posture? And what do you notice about your facial expression when you are in the mode of your Anxious Self? You might like to record your thoughts in the space provided in your *Personal Practice Workbook*.

What does the Anxious Self want to do? What are its behavioural urges or *actions*? Remember to consider the urges or fantasies of the Anxious Self, as well as the actions that are often taken. And consider too the way that the actions of the Anxious Self are often designed to create safety. Anxious Self is a mode that is safety seeking, and this is often reflected in the associated actions.

There are four main actions of the Anxious Self. Firstly, submission and an attempt to appease the other person in order to avoid any further tension or conflict. Secondly, avoidance or escape, sometimes thought of as fleeing to get away from the vicinity of the threat or danger. Thirdly freezing which causes us to feel unable to speak or act, or feeling caught 'like a deer in the headlights'. Finally, we might just do something to avoid the feeling itself, such as creating a distraction or switching off.

We are often triggered by current events to revisit old feelings of anxiety, anger, or shame. This is an automatic response and quite unconscious. When the Anxious Self is activated, are there any *memories* of past experiences that come to mind? What are the most powerful memories you associate with anxiety, and how long ago were these anxious experiences?

And lastly, what do you do to cope, recover from, or *settle* the anxiety? What helps you to down-regulate the body and mind patterns of the Anxious Self?

Here's a worked example of the Anxious Self:

Motives	Things feel scary and I need to stay safe. I want to try to control things, so I won't face any unexpected dangers.
Thoughts	What if they don't care, what if they don't love me? What if something really bad is going to happen, and they leave me?
Body	I just feel sick to the stomach. My heart starts racing. I get all choked up and feel like I can't breathe properly.
Actions	I try to make them see me. I try to please them, and I stay silent for the longest time hoping it will all be okay. I become submissive.
Memories	I remember being desperate for my brother's approval, I just wanted to be his friend. But he always chose others over me.
Settle	I try to distract myself with social media, and I watch videos about Greek and Roman history.

Sad Self

The third most common of the multiple selves is the Sad Self. Sadness can be particularly problematic and so as we consider the Sad Self, it is important to pace yourself in a way that feels comfortable so as not to become too overwhelmed. It's also important to distinguish sadness from the experience of depression.

The Sad Self is activated by experiences of loss and grief. This can be triggered by personal loss, relational loss, or material loss. It can also be triggered empathically in response to another person's loss, or even a loss depicted in a movie or book. Sadness is a very normal response to the loss of something we value, and the level of pain we feel is often directly related to how much emotional value we placed on that which was lost.

Depression is a much more multifaceted experience that may involve sadness but also involves hopelessness, helplessness, fatigue, disturbance to sleep and appetite, poor concentration and number of other criteria. This distinction between sadness and depression is important as we work towards being able to differentiate between patterns of the body and the mind. Here we will be specifically exploring sadness and the activation of Sad Self. So let's explore some of the same questions as before.

While it can sometimes be difficult to identify, we still want to consider what is the *motive* of Sad Self. Reflecting once again on the difficult interpersonal situation, what is it that triggered your sadness, and what did your Sad Self want? What would have been a good outcome from the point of view of Sad Self? What function does Sad Self play? Perhaps there is something that Sad Self is seeking, or perhaps defending against. It is worth considering what we feel might happen if the Sad Self was no longer present.

Regarding the many and varied *thoughts*, there is often a theme related to loss even though it may not be something you can easily identify. Loss can, of course, activate both Angry Self and Anxious Self, but differentiating these and seeing the sadness present can be very powerful and therapeutic. Another theme that can be a part of Sad Self is one of disconnection, either from yourself or others. The topic of sadness might also touch upon being alone or loneliness, even abandonment.

What thoughts go through your mind when Sad Self is activated? What ideas do you notice about loss, grief, or disconnection? Do you notice that you get stuck on certain thoughts? What ideas continue to trouble you, even after the situation that started it all is over? What do you think the other person is thinking in this situation? How might they feel about loss, grief, or disconnection?

What sorts of *bodily sensations* do you notice when your Sad Self is activated? How do your body, limbs, facial expression change when Sad Self is activated? Where is sadness located in the body and, if you could see it, what does Sad Self look like?

What are the behaviours urges and *actions* of the Sad Self? What does Sad Self want to do? What actions do you take when Sad Self is activated, and does Sad Self have fantasies about what it would like to do? You might like to record your thoughts in the space provided in your *Personal Practice Workbook*.

Several types of behavioural urges or actions are related to Sad Self. People can withdraw and isolate themselves, and avoid others for fear of bursting into tears or falling apart. People can also feel very lost and confused. And people can try to avoid feeling sad by distracting themselves.

Feelings of overwhelming sadness can feel quite scary and leave us feeling vulnerable. When we are sad we cry, we can't see, our noses get snotty, we can't smell or breathe, we feel weak and fatigued and have no energy to run or fight off a threat. Often sadness makes us feel far too vulnerable to external threats, and sometimes it can feel more energising and therefore better to be angry or even anxious.

When reflecting on the Sad Self pattern, what *memories* come to mind? Are there memories that you associate with being sad that are particularly powerful? How long ago did the experiences associated with the memories occur?

How do you respond in order to *settle* sadness? What helps you to regulate it, or cope with it? Some may be helpful, such as physical activity or talking with a friend, and some may be unhelpful, such as binge eating or drinking too much. What seems to settle sadness for you?

Here's a worked example of the Sad Self:

Motives	I just want to be loved and cared for, and to feel truly understood.
Thoughts	I'm so alone, always so alone. Nothing ever seems to go right for me. I'm so lonely.
Body	I feel really weak at the knees, almost like I am going to collapse in a heap. I feel heavy all over. And I cry.
Actions	I withdraw, go to my room, disappear. And I wait for someone to come and comfort me, but no one ever does.

Memories	When I was a child, I spent a lot of time alone, in my room, reading, or sometimes just sitting there alone until it gradually got dark and I went to sleep.
Settle	For me it's just easier to give up and resign myself to being alone. When I watch the videos about history, I find that I eventually settle down.

Understanding our own multiplicity: Is there anything else?

Most of us can identify our prominent emotions very easily but our experiences are much more complex, and reflecting on what else might be there can be very illuminating.

For example, during an argument, there may be anger on the surface, but sadness just below it. Or sadness may be the more obvious emotion, but there is anger beneath. Disentangling these separate responses is useful because a person who often responds with anger may discover that it's their sadness that they really need to work with.

Mind mapping, in which you separate out all the possible emotions you may have experienced, is a powerful way to help you identify the root causes of your suffering. Reflecting on any situation that caused you pain, start with the most prominent emotion, explore it thoroughly, and understand its motives. Then ask yourself the question, 'Is there anything else?'

Go under, over and around your more obvious emotions and see what else you can find. You may find it helpful to assume a compassionate posture and breathing rate while doing this exercise of discernment. Space is provided in your *Personal Practice Workbook* for this exercise.

- Is it anger, frustration, irritation, annoyance, resentment, or rage?
- Is it anxiety, worry, nervousness, apprehension, fear, or panic?
- Is it sadness, disappointment, despondency, grief, or despair?
- Or is it one or more of the many other nuanced descriptors related to the emotional categories of anger, anxiety, or sadness?
- Or is it embarrassment, humiliation, guilt or shame?

When the Selves are in Conflict

As we already know, humans have very complex brains! While we might have different body and brain patterns activated in any given situation, represented by multiple selves, we can also experience these selves as in conflict with one another.

Imagine the prehistoric human walking through the forest. Suddenly, they hear a rustle in the bushes. The first thing to happen is the activation of their threat system — 'This might be something that could eat me!' They immediately experience the emergence of the Anxious Self which is motivated by threat protection, as well as a pounding heart and the behavioural urge to flee. But almost simultaneously they might have the activation of the drive system. 'That could be something I could eat!' This leads to feeling motivated by hunger satiation, and an urge to dive into the bushes to catch their next meal.

These different patterns are in conflict with each other. Does our prehistoric human dive in and catch the meal, or do they run like the wind and get the heck out of there? If the source of the rustle were clearer, then the choice would be more apparent, but without knowing what's hiding in the bushes, this person would feel confused, disorganised and stuck! Eat/run, eat/run, eat/run? This internal conflict can be very painful, and can lead to feeling immobilised.

This same type of conflict can happen to us. Think of a university student who feels driven to get a high grade in their exams, but also feels terrified of failing, and instead ends up with a very clean house! Or imagine an old man who lives alone who is troubled by symptoms of forgetfulness — he may be too afraid to go to a doctor so drinks a few extra beers every night to make himself feel calmer. Both these people are stuck, and distract themselves so as to be free of the pain of conflict. But, of course, it can be more complex than this, especially when some of the multiple selves mentioned above are the ones in conflict.

Reflect once again on the difficult situation you just thought about. When you consider the respective selves you have differentiated, what do each of the selves think or feel about each of the others? What does Angry Self think and feel about Anxious Self and Sad Self? What does

Anxious Self think and feel about Angry Self and Sad Self? And what does Sad Self think and feel about Angry Self and Anxious Self?

Then go a little further in your self-examination. What are the specific angry feelings of this Angry Self about this Anxious Self? Is it frustration or irritation, is it contempt or deprecation, is it rage or fury? And what are the specific feelings Anxious Self has about Angry Self? Is Anxious Self frightened by Angry Self, fearful of what Angry Self might do and the consequences of that?

A common conflict between Angry Self and Anxious Self is that Angry Self thinks Anxious Self is weak and gutless, and therefore feels hostile contempt towards Anxious Self. Conversely, Anxious Self is scared to death about what Angry Self might do and the terrible negative consequences that might create.

Understanding all these nuances allows us to have a better understanding of ourselves and the work that we need to do. We are not just one emotion or one person; we are multiples. We have multiple selves which have arisen from activation of an evolved threat system. Once again, this is not our fault, but it is our responsibility to learn how to manage these different aspects of our human nature in order to be more compassionate to ourselves and others.

The good news is that our different aspects don't just relate to the very difficult or painful emotions, but can relate to a whole range of positive emotions as well. The joyful self, the determined self, the competitive self, the contented self, even the seductive self are all examples of the varied multiple selves that exist in any one person.

Compassion allows us to wisely understand the motives, thoughts and feelings of all our selves, and with strength and commitment, work towards integration. It also helps to remind us that other people are just like us and struggle with the same internal conflicts and desires.

Bringing the Compassionate Self to Emotional Integration

Arguments and conflict, challenges and tests, disappointments and losses, are all likely to trigger our threat system activation and a variety of responses from our multiplicity of selves. These multiple selves push and pull us in a variety of directions, sometimes in unison and sometimes opposing each other.

But we don't want these threat-based selves to be running the show! While they have a range of evolved benefits in helping us stay alive, they also come with a range of trade-offs. Anger can destroy relationships and get us into trouble, sadness can cause us pain and isolation, while anxiety can affect our health and social wellbeing.

So, to help negate these adverse outcomes, we need to activate our Compassionate Self.

When dealing with multiple selves, a calm mind thinks differently, so aligning our physiology with compassion is a very important first step.

Once again, we must bring it back to the body. Find a comfortable position, create a compassionate posture, and bring warm-friendliness to your facial expression. Remember our method acting approach, where we let the body take the lead role as our Compassionate Self. We need to ensure a friendly quality to the way we speak or address ourselves, even in our own self-talk. And finally, we want to bring attention to our breath, and settle into a soothing rhythm.

Take a few moments now to activate the physiological systems of the Compassionate Self.

We remember the *wisdom* we hold about our human brain; we understand that our old brains are very reactive, and our new brains get us caught in loops. We accept the randomness of our lives while taking responsibility to manage our responses so that we can be helpful rather than harmful to ourselves and others.

Next, we recall our strength and courage, that solid sense of being grounded, stable, determined, and able to respond to whatever might happen next. Compassion can manifest as friendliness and kindness, but more importantly, it has the components of strength and courage that enables us to take helpful action.

The Compassionate Self doesn't give up but draws on wisdom, strength and courage to keep going. It commits us to being helpful, supportive, kind, validating, encouraging, and reassuring when suffering presents itself.

In the case of multiple selves, the Compassionate Self allows us to pause, bring wisdom and understanding to the various brain and body patterns that are within us all. The Compassionate Self brings empathy to these different selves, as well as the motives and intentions of these different selves in a nonjudgmental way.

The Compassionate Self is also aware that the different selves, such as Angry Self, Anxious Self, or Sad Self, might not act to protect us skillfully or effectively. Often these different selves act in pre-programmed, reactive ways. The Compassionate Self helps us to step out of autopilot and choose to respond in ways that are more constructive.

Let's now reflect on the Compassionate Self and its perspective on the interpersonally challenging situation that you have considered above.

Firstly, explore the *motives* of the Compassionate Self. With respect to your challenging situation, what does the Compassionate Self want? What would be a good outcome for your Compassionate Self? What might be the function of your Compassionate Self? What is the suffering that the Compassionate Self would like to alleviate?

Secondly, what *thoughts* come to mind when you look at the situation from the perspective of the Compassionate Self? What does the Compassionate Self think about it? What about from the point of view of your guiding principles? What does the Compassionate Self think about the moment of conflict and the whole situation from a longer-term point of view?

Often the Compassionate Self is able to see the different perspectives of all involved — that includes you, your multiple selves, the other person, and their multiple selves! Even when there is a situation only involving two people, there are still many perspectives to take into account. The Compassionate Self has the wisdom to do this.

Because it can sometimes feel a little threatening to consider the mind of another person with whom you have a conflict, be aware that doing so can further trigger your threat-based patterns. You might even hear your Angry Self lash out with, 'Yeah, but it's all their fault, they are awful!' Luckily, your Compassionate Self has the ability to carefully navigate these different perspectives with sensitivity, empathy, and non-judgment.

Looking at challenging situations from a wider point of view we can also incorporate the idea of the flows of compassion: from you to the other, from you to yourself, and possibly from the other to you. While we can determine our own response, we cannot control whether the other person involved in a difficult interpersonal situation is likely to be compassionate towards us.

We are working all the time to create a compassionate posture, facial expression, voice tone, and soothing rhythm to our breath. But where in your body do you feel your compassion? Is it in your chest, your hands, your forehead? Knowing where you feel compassion in your body can be very useful to identify.

Note that compassion produces very different *bodily sensations* to other emotions. Often it's an interesting combination of down-regulation and solidity, although it depends on the situation you are facing. Sometimes compassionate action does require physiological up-regulation, such as a person sprinting to the water to save a child in distress. But often it feels like a calm resolve.

What *actions* does the Compassionate Self want to take? If the Compassionate Self could do anything right now, in order to be helpful rather than harmful, what would it do? The Compassionate Self might decide that some form of empathic listening might be the best option. This aspect of our conscious mind is more interested in cooperation and reconciliation and wants to move the situation away from aggression and competition.

The Compassionate Self is concerned with understanding any negative effects we might be having on others. As you can imagine, this takes presence of mind, self-awareness and a whole lot of courage. It might mean admitting to our own behaviour, which could result in guilty feelings for what we have done and the effects we have had. But it can be absolutely worth doing and crucial to changing the trajectory of the situation.

The Compassionate Self is also in a position to assess a situation and help guide you as to whether you should stay or leave a relationship. It's never easy to do so whether it's your partner, family member or a friend. But the Compassionate Self is not going to allow harm to continue happening to you; it will want you to have strong, healthy boundaries regarding the behaviour of others, especially where they are being unreasonable, insensitive, or downright abusive. Compassion can help you with the wisdom, strength and courage to move on from very difficult or toxic people, but still without hate or ongoing enmity.

Start to reflect on the *memories* you have of giving or receiving compassion or being compassionate towards yourself. What are some examples of times when others were compassionate towards you? How did that feel? What about some times you were compassionate to someone else? How did you feel? The Compassionate Self is able to draw on those experiences to further develop the wisdom of compassion and the confidence that it can be truly helpful. These kinds of memories can also be useful guides when deciding what to do.

Finally, we want insight into how our Compassionate Self might further *grow* and become increasingly embodied in our daily lives. Evolution has bestowed on us the capacity for compassion, but we can also consider how we can further cultivate that aspect of ourselves. What do you think would help your Compassionate Self grow? You might like to record your thoughts in the space provided in your *Personal Practice Workbook*.

Here's a worked example of the Compassionate Self:

Motives	I want to connect, cooperate, find a resolution that works for everyone, be helpful rather than harmful, and prevent harm happening to me.
Thoughts	It's okay. You can get to a place of agreement. It's difficult for both of you. These kinds of arguments are common. Just take stock and do your best.
Body	I feel calm but strong. I feel it in my arms and legs, stabilising me, helping me to feel grounded. And my body feels slowed down, but optimistic.
Actions	I take a few soothing breaths, try to really listen to the other person, try to understand them, try to express my perspective as kindly and clearly as possible

Memories I remember when this has worked before with this person. When we are calm with each other, and genuinely listening, things usually work out okay.

Grow   I have learned many things, and this is a chance to practice it and hopefully it will start to come to mind when I need it most.

Ryan

Ryan was an impressive guy. He was in his late thirties and already highly successful in his field of work, having lived and worked internationally at global companies. He'd taken a bit of a hit lately though and had become burnt out in the high octane, high competition environment of the company he worked at overseas. Then he lost his mother quite unexpectedly, prompting him to return home. When I saw him, he was working again and had set himself up in a nice apartment, but he was very sad, and his Sad Self was exhausted, unenthusiastic, and especially pessimistic.

We had worked together for a number of sessions when we started to explore his multiple selves. We had identified this Sad Self, which we called his 'pessimistic self'. His pessimistic self was very clear about what it believed: 'Don't want anything because you probably won't get it.' We had also identified his critical self, that part of him that berated his pessimistic self with 'You're pathetic,' 'Stop whining,' and 'Just get on with it,' all said in a very hostile tone.

So, having explored his pessimistic self and his critical self, we then used an imagery exercise to begin to activate his Compassionate Self. We started with the body practices, his posture, facial expression and soothing rhythm breathing, and then I asked him to imagine a safe place, and being visited there by his ideal compassionate other. I prompted the wisdom, strength, courage, and kindness of compassion, as well as the ideal compassionate other's commitment to be helpful, rather than harmful, where ever possible. And then I asked him to imagine the compassionate other wanted to tell him something, something that was just what he needed to hear right now in his life. Just to listen to what the compassionate other had come to say.

After the exercise was finished, we discussed what that experience was like for him. He said, 'It was too difficult. When you talked about the qualities of compassion, I couldn't think of anyone who is really like that.

And I couldn't think of any compassionate words. There is no solution; nothing is going to change, I'm never going to feel any different. I just don't think this is going to work.'

Can you guess what happened at that moment for Ryan? Exactly! This was the return again of the pessimistic self. Working with multiple selves isn't easy. There isn't an easy or obvious separation between them, and they spill in and out of each other. So it takes reflection, and practice, and developing the skills to be validating, reassuring and encouraging towards yourself. Ryan did eventually get there with effort and his Compassionate Self became a strong ally in his recovery. You can get there too!

And So Begins the Conversation

Our different selves are constantly in conversation with each other. Sometimes they agree and sometimes they don't, but they never stop talking. It's very important to understand the motives of our different multiple selves as this can be crucial to mastering ourselves. For example, we might be a person whose anger overpowers our anxiety and results in aggressive conduct, or our anxiety overpowers anger and results in submissive behaviour.

This underlying process, however, is also to our great advantage. We can bring the Compassionate Self to the conversation and, using the quality of empathy, see if we can start to understand our multiple selves. A great way to describe this is mentalising — this usually refers to being able to imagine the mind of another person, but in this context, it can be imagining the mind, motives, thoughts and feelings of the different selves. The Compassionate Self is well-placed to consider things from the perspective of the other selves. Your *Personal Practice Workbook* provides space for you to record your thoughts as you consider the perspectives of your multiple selves.

Let's start with the Angry Self. Imagine you are in the role of the Compassionate Self. What does your Compassionate Self make of the Angry Self? Describe its posture, facial expression and voice tone, and the way you see Angry Self behave. How would you like to try to help the Angry Self?

Now let's consider the Anxious Self. Once again, from the perspective of the Compassionate Self, what do you make of your Anxious Self? Describe the posture, facial expression and voice tone, and the way the Anxious Self behaves. What would you like to do or say to help the Anxious Self?

Do the same exercise for your Sad Self. Describe your Sad Self from the perspective of the Compassionate Self, and what you would like to do or say to help.

You may notice that the Compassionate Self is a benevolent part of you, much like an ideal parent, mentor or therapist might be. It combines the wisdom, strength and courage and commitment with being helpful, supportive, and caring. The Angry Self, the Anxious Self, and the Sad Self tend to be much more self-focused, and motivated by threat system activation. The Compassionate Self is a shift in motivation, one that is driven to be helpful.

The Compassionate Self doesn't get into arguments or fights with the multiple selves, nor does it pity or patronise them. Instead, the Compassionate Self remains nonjudgmental, validates the thoughts and feelings of the multiple selves, and provides comfort and support. It encourages them to try something new, so they can still meet their motives in constructive ways.

Validation. Reassurance. Encouragement.

It is through this process that the multiple selves, previously differentiated and regarded as separate parts, can be integrated and invited in with their various valuable contributions. The multiple selves become a team working together for the greatest good.

While it may be tempting to think it would be easier to get rid of aspects of ourselves we find unhelpful, every part of ourselves has something important to offer. Even anger can be constructive. We need to understand and integrate the Angry Self so it can be most helpful, and least harmful, to ourselves and others. So too, with respect to the

Anxious Self and Sad Self. When we bring them onboard, our lives can really start to transform.

My Story

> From my experience as a therapist, some of the most powerful work we can do is chair work. This involves having multiple chairs, one for each of the multiple selves, and moving about the room, from chair to chair, taking the perspectives of each self in turn. Chair-work allows us to literally begin a conversation between the multiple selves, including bringing the Compassionate Self to the conversation.
>
> Tobyn Bell is a psychotherapist from the UK who specialises in compassion focused therapy and the use of chair work. He has presented extensively around the world and has published important research on the topic. Some of his recent work has found that getting into the role of each of the selves, truly embodying each one in turn, can have a powerful impact and facilitates real change for people undertaking compassion focused therapy.
>
> Given how powerful chair work can be, it can be very helpful to do this kind of work with a therapist so that you have the right support to make the most out of the experience.

Three Pearls

This chapter has introduced the idea of multiple selves, such a crucial aspect when working in a compassion-focused way, and lots to remember! Keep note of three pearls from this chapter in your *Personal Practice Workbook*.

Chapter 8

Working with Self-Criticism

When the Critic Joins the Conversation

We're all very familiar with the little voice inside our heads which is offering us 'feedback'. We are not always aware it's there, but it's rarely quiet, and while this Critical Self can be constructive, it can also be harsh, mean and hostile, reaching the point of self-attacking, self-blaming, and self-hating.

The other day I was leaving the house and, like many people, was rehearsing to myself 'wallet, keys, phone, wallet, keys, phone etc.' I'm not sure what went wrong, perhaps I was in a rush, but by the time I reached the car I realised I'd forgotten my keys.

'You bloody idiot! What is wrong with you? You loser!'

At that moment, I suddenly became aware of my critical voice. I thought, 'Hang on a sec, that's a bit harsh!' On this occasion I was fortunate that I noticed the Critical Self immediately. But as awful as the critical voice sounds, this is very common. On most days there can be several occasions when we attack ourselves, whether it be for something quite minor or something more significant. Whatever our perceived failing, the inner critic can be ruthless.

Iminathi

Iminathi was a young woman whose family had arrived some years before from Africa. She had completed all of her high school here and was now at university studying international relations. But she was having a very hard time with her confidence and self-worth. In fact, she came along to see me because she was starting to feel overwhelmed by anxiety and depression, her studies were a real struggle, and she was becoming more and more withdrawn and isolated.

She was a very driven woman and had strong values around social justice, as well as a dream to do good work in her community and around the world. She really wanted to help people. However, the more we talked, the more we realised that her drive often spilled into perfectionism. She would set herself unrelenting and unachievable standards, which meant that she never felt like she had succeeded. She always felt like she had failed. We worked out together that her drive and threat systems were overlapping — a mixture of drive to succeed and fear of failing.

During one session, I tried to explore her personal strengths and qualities so that we could affirm those and build confidence. Together we came up with a number of great qualities, such as strong, caring, experienced, clever, hard-working, determined, brave, and compassionate. It was a slow-paced conversation, carefully exploring, evoking, suggesting this list of qualities. Gradually, it seemed like she was taking them onboard.

As the session drew to an end, Iminathi said something that really cut through, and helped us realise a key source of her distress. She said, 'Maybe I am those things. I'm definitely determined to do good things for my people. But do you really think I am a good person? Putting aside my disgusting face, of course.'

There it was, the self-hating, self-loathing self-criticism. This Critical Self became such an important focus in our work from then on, not only to do with her appearance but across the spectrum of her intelligence and personality.

It's such a strange phenomenon. We would never speak to anyone else in the way we sometimes berate ourselves. So why the harsh treatment? Well, as I am sure you have guessed, the Critical Self too has its origins in our complex brains and in the ways we have evolved to survive.

The Mixed Blessing of Self-Monitoring

Self-critical thinking begins with our ability to monitor and evaluate ourselves. To criticise something in ourselves, we first must turn our attention to it. Did I say something stupid? Do I have body odour?

Humans are specialists in this kind of self-monitoring. The Labrador losing his winter coat could not care less that he's looking shaggy and bedraggled, he just runs around as happy as ever. Other animals don't monitor their appearance, intelligence or personality as we do, and therefore, as far as we know, they don't critically attack themselves.

Self-monitoring can be very useful — all animals monitor pain, hunger, temperature and fatigue, and then respond accordingly. Even systems humans have created follow a similar pattern. Our cars monitor how much petrol is left in the tank, and the light comes on to let us know it's time to fill up, or a smoke alarm alerts us to when its battery is running out of charge.

This is the basic function of self-monitoring: to check how the system is operating and respond accordingly, so that it operates properly, efficiently and enduringly. The human brain is also a system that self-monitors — however, it does so in very complex ways and, as we shall see, with a number of difficult trade-offs.

Every moment we are monitoring ourselves and changing our conduct accordingly. Just think of the moment-to-moment checking and adjusting that we do during even the simplest conversations. Do I understand them properly? Am I expressing myself adequately? Back and forth it goes.

We constantly monitor our physiological state, our emotional state, our behaviours and that of others, how we might compare to them and how they might be receiving us. Our observations and self-judgment are influenced by our experiences, including those from our childhood. If a parent always expressed angry disappointment when we didn't succeed academically, then it's likely we have internalised that response and will judge ourselves harshly in this same regard.

While self-monitoring makes sense from an evolutionary point of view to keep us safe and stable, how does self-criticism arise? And how do these patterns become embedded in our thinking?

The Elusive Ideal Self

We all have an ideal version of ourselves and who we would like to be. For a long time, I wanted to be a rock star, but sadly, it never happened! That may be a flippant example, but in very real ways we all have a sense of the ideal version of ourselves in any given moment: the perfect score, the perfect comeback, or the ideal entrance to a social event. Unfortunately, there is usually a mismatch between this ideal self and the person we actually are, between the expectations and the actual experience. This is sometimes referred to as the *disappointment gap*.

When the ideal self is focused on being competent or successful, the actual self seems less competent, less successful, and therefore a failure. When the ideal self is fixated on being well-liked or popular, the actual self feels rejected and isolated. When the ideal self concentrates on physical appearance and attractiveness, the actual self feels ugly and unwanted. These are all examples of the disappointment gap.

The ideal self is aspirational, while the actual self is threat-focused — the intensity of the disappointment between the two is a function of the severity of the feared consequences of the actual self. Or, in other words, the greater the gap, the deeper the disappointment.

Ultimately the threat we feel is to our social rank and the fear of losing status, and being criticised, shamed, rejected and isolated. The disappointment gap then triggers self-attacking. Name-calling, 'should' statements, and self-deprecation start to roll off the tongue, literally and metaphorically. And so arrives the Critical Self.

The Different Forms of Self-Criticism

Often the Critical Self is a mixture of emotions, some of which might be derived from other aspects of the self, but always directed at the self. Anger, sadness, hatred and contempt can influence the emotional quality of the Critical Self, but of course, self-criticism can vary in tone and quality.

Some people believe that even though they might be competent, effective or good, they feel they could and should do better. This is a kind of *self-improvement* style of self-criticism. A classic example of this might be a professional golfer who has a deep belief in themselves and their own ability but becomes aware that a part of their game has slightly deteriorated and needs work. In this case, their criticism is aimed at self-improvement and can be quite motivating.

For others, a long-standing and persistent sense of inferiority and inadequacy creates a feeling that they should do better, but without a core sense of being fundamentally okay. For people with this sense of *inadequate self*, there is a need to make up for these inadequacies, and yet a constant sense that they cannot overcome their own failings. Consequently, chronic self-criticism arises. Their greatest fear is making mistakes, being found out and subsequently shamed. This inferiority or inadequacy is very painful and constantly drives self-criticism.

For quite a number of people, the function of their self-criticism is not about wanting to improve, nor is it about avoiding making mistakes or being shamed by others, but rather it is about a core self-hatred. They loathe themselves or certain aspects of who they are. The *hated self* can be so intense that, rather than improving aspects of themselves, they actually want to be rid of those aspects, or expunge them from their being. They might feel disgust towards aspects of themselves, abhorring how they look, speak, act, or relate. The pain of self-hatred can be constant and unrelenting.

My Story

> Dr Chris Irons is a UK clinical psychologist who has been researching and writing about self-criticism and compassion focused therapy for many years. A close collaborator to Professor Paul Gilbert, Dr Irons' research has focused on understanding the forms and functions of self-criticism. He has done foundational work to help us understand the type of self-criticism that may be helpful and the type that may be unhelpful. Sometimes the function is to help us improve, but sometimes self-criticism can serve to hurt and harm ourselves for our perceived failures.
>
> Sometimes we believe our self-criticism is designed to help us improve, but the quality or tone of our self-criticism becomes quite unwittingly harmful instead. Dr Irons' work reminds us to carefully consider our own self-criticism and whether we can be self-critical in self-correcting ways, or whether the quality and tone of our self-criticism becomes

self-attacking, self-hating and ultimately very unhelpful and even harming of ourselves.

So, How Did Self-Criticism Evolve?

You might ask why on earth self-criticism evolved, but we have to consider again some of the evolutionary information presented earlier, and remember what the core threat is for human beings. The greatest fear for all of us is to find ourselves alone; our very survival depends on others, so a lot is at stake if we are rejected, abandoned or cast out of the group. Being alone could mean death. And as we know, our fundamental evolutionary adaptive question is, how do we avoid that?

> *I must avoid being cast out of the group at all costs.*

It makes sense that we self-monitor social position, status, rank, standing, and especially to notice when we are on a downward trajectory. There is no point noticing our wins or successes, or our social triumphs — we have to be aware of the moments when we fail because those are the moments that put us at most risk of rejection and abandonment.

This is an important point with respect to self-criticism. While on the surface it might appear that we have superficial concerns about being regarded as a failure, unattractive or disliked, we need to remember that behind all of this is the core fear of being alone. Our self-monitoring, self-judging and self-attacking have developed because of this evolved fear of the ultimate consequences of being alone.

The Functions of Self-Criticism

Self-criticism is a human brain function of social threat monitoring, and these functions can vary, depending on life experiences. Again, we see that we are born with an evolved brain that we don't get to choose, and are shaped by a range of life experiences which influence the functions of self-criticism.

Imagine a child who has very intimidating parents. This child might have often been on the receiving end of blame, while the parents never took responsibility for their own conduct or its impact. This child might learn a self-blaming style of self-criticism in response to people they find overpowering. The function of this blame and anger turned inward towards oneself is as a safety strategy to avoid the social consequences of being rejected or abandoned.

Or consider a child who is incessantly bullied and comes to the conclusion that if only they were better or different, then they wouldn't have to suffer. They become disappointed with themselves and who they are and in turn they become very self-critical. Again, the function is to keep themselves socially safe, although such self-criticism can also keep them in a submissive and subordinate social status, which then entraps them in bullying and rejection.

Some people may have had a mother or father who constantly criticised them: 'You're stupid…you're weak…toughen up!' Sometimes these kinds of comments are repeated so often that they become ingrained in the child's psyche like an internalised voice. Even as adults, the echoes of these critical remarks continue like an incessant commentary on that person's life. Being able to recognise and distinguish these voices can be very important.

It is usually the more global self-hating self-criticism that does the most damage. Being critical of specific attributes can be more directed towards self-improvement, whereas a more comprehensive, global attack can be much more harmful. When the criticism is tainted with anger, contempt, and disgust, then it is more likely to lead to real difficulties, especially in terms of mood and mental health.

The How and Why of Your Self-Criticism

Now, before you say, 'But I'm never self-critical,' let's just see. The difficulty is opening up to the self-critical part of ourselves that is probably there just under the surface; the harshest, meanest, most disparaging things we say to ourselves. And the contempt that can go along with it.

To start with: your ideal self. Spend a few moments reflecting on your Ideal Self and make notes in your *Personal Practice Workbook*.

What are some of the ideals you have about the way you would like to be? What do you wish you were better at? What would be great about being your ideal self? What do you think might happen if you can't achieve that?

What about in the moments when you don't achieve this ideal self? What happens when you don't achieve these ideals, when you fall short, when you are disappointed, frustrated or annoyed at yourself?

Think about what is behind this need to be the ideal self. What are you really frightened of, if you don't achieve these ideals? What would be so bad if you weren't able to be your ideal self in any given situation?

Remember that we are often familiar with our more immediate fears, such as failure or being unattractive, but we always like to get behind those and see what the core fears might be. These fears are usually meaningful from an evolutionary point of view and are especially connected to social threat or injury, and the fear of being alone and vulnerable. While self-criticism often sounds very nasty, it is there to defend us against this core fear that human beings have long held, generation after generation, millennia after millennia.

So, turning to the Critical Self, what sorts of things do you think or say to yourself when you are critical like that? What do you tell yourself when the Critical Self is running the show?

What are the feelings of the Critical Self when it's telling you these things? The words are one thing, but when they are delivered with emotional qualities of anger, hostility, contempt or disdain, they can be much more painful.

How does the Critical Self feel in the body? What are the bodily sensations you feel when your Critical Self is activated? What posture does your body shift into? How does your facial expression appear? How does your voice tone sound?

In Chapter 1 we spoke about the three emotion regulation systems: the threat system, the drive system, and the soothing-affiliative system. Which of these three systems seems most activated as part of the Critical Self? Are you feeling more socially connected, which would suggest soothing system activation, or are you feeling more social disconnected, which might suggest the threat system?

A vicious cycle starts to develop at this point. The Critical Self is largely emerging from the threat system, via fears of social threat or injury, and is acting in order to defend the self from injury. However, the position the Critical Self goes on to take, namely the mean, harsh and hostile treatment of the self, is further threat system activating! In the end, we are receiving the kind of treatment from ourselves that we originally feared from others. We have such tricky brains!

It can be useful at this point to reflect on the origins of our self-criticism. Be aware that this can be a revealing, but also difficult process. For example, when we trace back our self-criticism, we often arrive at quite painful memories of experiences early in our life. This can relate to experiences with key people, such as parents, teachers and friends. It can sometimes relate to experiences of mistreatment or abuse by trusted adults, including verbally, physically and sexually. Sometimes very complex trauma is the origin of our own self-criticism, and this might be best processed through face-to-face therapy or treatment.

If you would prefer not to explore the origins of your self-criticism on your own right now, skip this part of the book. However, if you feel able to consider your early life experiences for a moment, we will try to get a sense of how the Critical Self has developed. So, if it's okay with you, we are now going to explore the origins of your self-criticism.

When were some of the earliest times your self-criticism was present for you? Do you remember what it was a reaction to? Was the origin of your self-criticism some kind of external source, such as others being angry, hostile and critical towards you? Or was it arising out of an internal source, such as your own disappointment or frustration? Rarely are we born harshly self-critical; usually something has happened along the way.

We live in a society which is hyper-competitive. Right from the start, successes are rewarded and failures are either ignored or punished. We are constantly comparing ourselves to others; the prevalence of selfies and social media has made this a global phenomenon. In some ways, the self-esteem movement has made that worse by tacitly encouraging us to focus on what is good about ourselves and how we are better than others.

It feels like there is so much riding on our success, and if we don't yet feel this pressure often our parents and teachers do on our behalf, and so they apply the criticism for us. We learn from them and adopt this attitude for ourselves. Add social media into the mix, even for children of a relatively young age, and we all have so much to compare ourselves with, so much to feel inferior to, and so much to make us feel incompetent.

Bearing in mind that we are such social creatures with brains that are extremely sensitive to social injury sometimes it's hard to believe we are ever nice to ourselves!

But I DO Make Mistakes!

We all make mistakes. We disappoint ourselves and we fail. We do not need to deny this or pretend it isn't so. It is important to take steps to learn from our mistakes and try to improve; this is another important need of our human psyche. It's not easy, but we do want to find a way to be less self-hating, contemptuous and disdainful of ourselves when we do make a mistake.

Instead, we want to activate the Compassionate Self, with its wisdom, strength, courage and commitment, to join the conversation again, and offer ourselves the help we need. Our mistakes usually aren't that bad, and failures really are okay. To be human is to be imperfect, and to be able to soften ourselves in response to our own imperfections is the path to a calm, peaceful, happy life.

We do need to know how to deal with things when they go wrong, like knowing how to change a car tire; learning what to do when things go wrong is liberating! We can feel more confident to go out, explore and grow. The alternative is to always be vigilantly self-monitoring and frightened, and then attacking ourselves when things go wrong. 'You idiot!' Self-criticism can make life far more difficult, with greater suffering than is necessary.

A Functional Analysis of Self-Criticism

Self-criticism comes in many different forms and has several functions. Sometimes people feel that it is helpful and drives them in a competitive way. At other times, however, it can become more hostile, vicious and self-hating.

The next step is to create an image of the Critical Self and how it appears for you, and then assess whether there is harm associated with self-hating or shame-based self-criticism. As you work through the process below, you may wish to write your thoughts and reflections in your *Personal Practice Workbook*.

Take a few moments to reflect on the ways in which you are self-critical. What do you think is the function of your self-criticism? What might happen if you were no longer self-critical? What are your greatest fears of losing your Critical Self?

I invite you now to sit comfortably and take a few soothing breaths to create a sense of strength and grounding. Now consider these questions quietly and slowly; perhaps briefly closing your eyes. Give yourself time to evaluate your answer and whenever you are ready, open your eyes again and write a few notes. Take as much time as you need.

You need not focus on anything too major to start with, perhaps something about which you feel mildly to moderately self-critical. Try to bring something specific to mind.

Breathing slowly and staying grounded, imagine that you can see the inner critic as something outside yourself with a form of its own. What does your critic look like? What do you notice about its body posture and facial expression? What words would you use to describe how the Critical Self looks?

By all means, make the notes as detailed and descriptive as you like.

Now that you can see or sense the critic has a particular form or presence, really listen to what it says. Let it speak to you without interfering or challenging it. Notice, too, how it speaks, its tone and general manner. Take a few moments to reflect on what the critic says.

Next, start to notice, what does the critic feel for you? What emotions is it feeling and expressing towards you? What does it want to do to you? And what sort of relationship does it want to have with you?

Now that you have observed and listened to your critic, how has this left you feeling in your body, in your mind?

Finally, sit quietly for a few moments taking a few deep breaths, and when you're ready, continue onto the next section.

Your Impressions of the Critical Self?

Do you believe this inner critic truly has your best interests at heart? Does it support and encourage you when things get tough or when you are failing? Does it take joy in your success or your wellbeing?

Does your inner critic appear before you do things? Does it warn you that you might not do them well, or does it encourage you?

After you have made a mistake, does your critical inner voice want to keep reminding you? Does it strengthen and inspire you to have another go?

Self-correction can be very helpful, depending on how it is delivered. But sometimes self-criticism makes things harder and make us less likely to achieve our goals. Given what it says about us, how it says it, and how it feels about us, self-criticism can be an undermining force. There is an alternative approach, one that involves more compassionate encouragement and self-correction.

Cultivating Compassionate Encouragement

There is a part of you that also wants you to have drive, motivation and aspirations, to live according to your values. This is a compassionate part, based on insight, wisdom, strength and courage, and commitment. Let's now spend some time exploring this part of you and the function of compassionate encouragement. Again, space is provided in your *Personal Practice Workbook* for making notes as you work through this new exercise.

Once again, let's begin to activate the Compassionate Self. Assume the compassionate posture, with back upright, shoulders back and chest open. Take a few soothing breaths, breathing in for a count of five and out for a count of five. Bring a warm and friendly expression to your face and with each out-breath, say silently to yourself, 'mind slowing down, body slowing down.' Settle into this present moment.

Now consider your Compassionate Self, the part of you that is kind, strong, wise and courageous. This self has non-judgmental acceptance and empathic understanding; it is sympathetically moved by suffering and motivated by a care for wellbeing to offer help, while also being able to tolerate feelings of distress.

The Compassionate Self has a deep commitment to addressing suffering wherever it can; however, we have to learn and practice, seeking just what would be most helpful. The compassionate voice is a friendly and helpful voice because it recognises that life is difficult.

Next, consider the perspective of your Compassionate Self. What are the greatest wishes your Compassionate Self has for you? What aspirations does the Compassionate Self have for you? What would it like you to achieve out of a genuine care for your wellbeing?

Now bring to mind again something about yourself which your inner voice often criticises.

Imagine that you could see the Compassionate Self as if that part of your mind could take a form of its own. What does your Compassionate Self look like? Really try to sense that form.

Now that you can see or sense the presence of your Compassionate Self allow it to speak to you. Let it say what it really wants to say about you and to you, and about the struggles you've had. Notice too how it addresses you, its voice tone and overall manner.

Now start to notice what emotions is it feeling and expressing towards you. What sort of relationship does it want to have with you?

Keeping in mind the issue you have been critical about, and now that you've listened carefully to the voice of your Compassionate Self, what does this leave you feeling now? In terms of your goals and aspirations, how are you feeling?

Finally, sit quietly for a few moments breathing deeply and, when you're ready, continue on.

Your Impressions of the Compassionate Self?

What did you notice about the Compassionate Self and its perspective on the thing you feel self-critical about? How did the Compassionate Self support or encourage you?

The Compassionate Self is encouraging, supportive and caring while self-criticism can be more undermining, uninspiring, deflating and de-motivating.

With the Compassionate Self, the values don't change, but the drivers change to compassionate encouragement and self-correction. We can find support in our Compassionate Self, and grow to be the person we want to be.

Bringing Compassion to the Critic

In the exercise above, we developed an understanding of the Critical Self, activated the Compassionate Self and created an image of how it might respond. We can see that while the Critical Self might be well-intended, it can also be de-motivating, while the Compassionate Self can be encouraging and self-correcting.

It's tempting to think that one way to solve this problem is to rid ourselves of the Critical Self. Unfortunately, that cannot be done. As much as we would prefer not to have a Critical Self, we do, and that's just part of being human.

But here's the clever thing. Just as we were able to differentiate the angry, anxious and sad selves and bring the Compassionate Self to those conversations, we can also differentiate the Critical Self and bring the Compassionate Self to that dialogue as well.

Remember the image of Critical Self from before? Imagine it's there in front of you now, doing what it does and being critical. Now you are watching it from the point of view of your Compassionate Self cultivating a compassionate motivation *towards the Critical Self*. This seems a little strange to suggest, but within your mind you now have the Compassionate Self holding the Critical Self with compassion.

The next step is to really engage your compassionate wisdom and try to 'look behind' the Critical Self and identify what's driving it. Remember, we know that what drives the inner critic is a fear of social threats and injuries, so perhaps you will see a fear of rejection, isolation, exclusion or inferiority. You might simply see that the Critical Self is frightened of not being wanted, not being loved. Perhaps there is a deeply felt anxiety of not belonging.

If you begin to feel that this is painful or distressing, always remember to bring it back to the body and the calming exercises we have used before. You can take it slowly, moving back and forth. Approach the Critical Self and if you begin to feel distressed, engage the Compassionate Self. When you feel ready, try again.

We want the Compassionate Self to see and understand these experiences without being drawn back into them and getting lost in anger, fear or sadness.

The next step is to really engage your compassionate strength and courage, and start to consider the origins of the Critical Self. What were those early life experiences, disappointments or hurts, things other people did or said that led to the beginnings of this Critical Self? Strength and courage are important here because this is tough stuff.

The Compassionate Self is strong and able to witness the Critical Self and all the hardship that might have led to its creation. Sadly, these very painful things do happen, human beings can do unpleasant things to each other; remember that most of us have suffered this way.

Finally, engage your compassionate commitment to be helpful, rather than harmful, to yourself. What would be most helpful here? What might you say to a friend or someone that you love who has fallen foul of all their self-criticism? In exactly the same way, your Compassionate Self can offer your Critical Self kindness, wisdom, support or comfort.

Perhaps the Compassionate Self could offer some gentle well-wishes to the Critical Self: *I'm sorry you are feeling this way. I'm sorry you are hurting. I understand. Whatever might be causing you to want to criticise me, and to say or feel those things towards me, I hope this will end, and you find peace.*

The key is that the Compassionate Self wants to understand the Critical Self; it wants to see behind the hostility and attack to the fear that drives it, and remain respectful, empathic, and committed to being helpful.

Three Pearls

Self-criticism is really tricky, but also really common. Hopefully, you are able to take a few key points from Chapter 8, and write them down as three pearls in your *Personal Practice Workbook*.

Chapter 9

Working with Shame

Introducing Shame

Shame is a very complex and problematic set of emotions that relate to a sense of social threat. Sometimes shame can lead to submissive behaviours, in which the person wants to flee, shy away, or hide. Just think of those moments where we feel shame. Our bodies slump or hunch over, we bow our heads and hold our faces in our hands, we blush or cry, and we feel terribly small. All we want to do is find a rock to hide under.

But sometimes shame can lead to something very different: aggression. In these instances, the experience of shame causes us to fight, lash out, or retaliate. Our complexion gets flushed and red, our muscles tighten all over, our faces contort in rage, and we verbally or physically strike out.

These are the two main ways that shame might be expressed: submission and aggression. Often, shame is a response to the power dynamics in any given situation. The more inferior or weak we feel in the social context, the more likely we are to respond in submissive ways. Conversely, the more secure and powerful we feel, the more likely we are to respond with aggression.

Like all things, we have our evolved, problematic brains to thank for all this! Shame, as a set of social-emotional experiences, is a result of human evolution and survival.

Think of ancient people living in family groups or tribes with scarce resources. People had to be very cooperative and share whatever was available with the group — there would have been strict rules around how this should be done. In this scenario, imagine the response when one day a member of the tribe takes more than their fair share — and gets discovered.

Suddenly that tribe member is exposed to significant social threat. If they are rejected or cast out of the group, then they will die; they cannot survive without the protection and goodwill of the group. They now have no power in the situation, and they respond with all the bodily responses described above. They feel they are a terrible, awful person, and they express that too. Because of their response, the tribe decides they are allowed to stay, but they are now much lower in social status, and the shame persists.

On another day, another member of the tribe does the same thing, but they already have a much higher social rank. This person is similarly shamed but they respond with aggression, threatening to harm or cast out others. The others then submit, fearing their power. However, the difference here is that this person's status has to be high enough for that individual to succeed. It's a risk because if there are enough people of power who can override the shamed person, then they will be defeated and cast out. Otherwise, they too will have to turn to submissive shame to stay. It's complex!

My Story

Dr Marcela Matos is a marvellous researcher from Universidade de Coimbra in Portugal who has made an enormous contribution to the research around shame and compassion. I had the great privilege to interview her for a podcast episode on The Compassion Initiative Podcast in which she described her research journey. But it was one brief comment from Dr Matos that beautifully summed up the dilemma of shame:

'If you're not valued in the eyes of others, then you won't be chosen to be their friend, partner, lover, so that represents a huge threat. So even though [shame] has this amazing adaptive evolutionary value, it comes with a lot of suffering.'

Humans have evolved to be particularly concerned with social threat, and so we become highly sensitive to how we might be viewed in the minds of others. Being concerned with, and managing, how we are viewed by others in the group makes evolutionary sense! But like many evolved adaptations of the human brain, shame certainly comes with some painful tradeoffs.

Shame is fundamentally a self-conscious or social emotion, driven by a fear of being rejected or experiencing other negative social consequences. Shame is an emotion that is primarily about how we are perceived in a social context. We also have positive self-conscious or social emotions, such as pride, a feeling of being admired or favoured in some way. However, shame really is the opposite of this and relates to when we believe others disapprove of us or we are out of favour.

Lastly, the emotion of shame is a global, pervasive, whole-self sense of ourselves. In other words, shame is not, 'I wish I was better at this or that,' but rather, 'I am bad, I am ugly, I am stupid, I am worthless, I am unlovable.' With shame, we have a globally negative view of ourselves.

Sophia

'I just can't leave the house,' said Sophia as her opening statement. 'It was bad enough just to get here today, that was almost impossible. I just panic!'

We started to talk about Sophia's anxiety and avoidance. She barely left her home, sometimes not venturing out for many days. She had lost touch with most friends, and she was reluctant to have much to do with her family, including her own children. Going to the shops was torturous, and when she did go, it was often late at night when she hoped nobody would be there. She hadn't seen a movie in a long time, and this was something she loved to do.

At first, I thought her core concern was the anxiety, perhaps panic and agoraphobia, but as we continued talking I noticed that her physical posture started to bow gradually. The first change was when she lost eye contact, turning her gaze to the floor. Then her shoulders gradually started to slump, and her head bowed lower. Slowly a hand came to her mouth, and then both hands we pressed against her cheeks. As she spoke, a flush started to rise up her neck and into her cheeks. She started to brightly blush, and then her face collapsed into her hands, covering her eyes.

'I'm just an awful person,' she said. 'I'm ugly and stupid, and I just can't face anyone. I know they're all judging me. They know. They can see right through me.' She paused for a moment, and I paused too, leaving just a little silence. Then she finished with one final, vitriolic declaration: 'I'm disgusting to the core.' That's when I finally realised that we needed to work with Sophia's shame.

What do They Think, What do I Think?

There are two main aspects to shame that are often highly correlated, yet also distinct; we refer to these as external and internal shame.

External shame relates to the feelings, thoughts and bodily responses we have if other people were to look down on us, disparage us, or view us with disdain. With external shame, the focus is on trying to identify what other people might be thinking and feeling about us, and what the consequences of their view might be. As such, a lot of energy is put into scanning the conduct or conversations of others to find clues about what they might be thinking.

Unfortunately, with external shame, we scan with our own individual filter, often ignoring any evidence that people like or value us, and instead only ever seeing evidence of their disdain. It's actually worse than that because through the filter of external shame we might even see neutral or positive behaviour as evidence of someone's dislike or disapproval: 'She's just pretending,' or 'He just wants something.'

Much of our feeling of external shame relates to our innate desire to be valued and to belong. In a sense, it is also about things like reputation and our social standing *in the minds of others*. The evolved human brain sees it as catastrophic, given the potential consequences, when we are devalued.

Just think of a secret you hold, something you ordinarily wouldn't want to share and imagine that secret got out. How would you feel and what would that mean for you? Most of us have had thoughts, feelings, urges, or desires, or even past conduct, that you have felt unable to express for fear of external shame. Everyone feels it to some degree.

> *External shame is when I believe that other people see me as inadequate, inferior, unworthy, and no good.*

The other aspect of shame that is important to consider is *internal shame*. There is often a lot of overlap between external and internal shame. Internal shame has its focus turned inwards, towards *what we think and feel about ourselves*. In the case of internal shame, it is the self judging the self. This is closely related to our discussion about self-criticism and is sometimes known as shame-based self-criticism.

> *Internal shame is when I see myself as inadequate, inferior, unworthy, and no good.*

The fear that drives the shame-based self-criticism and by association internal shame, is the fear of external shame, that is, being seen by others as no good and therefore abandoned and alone.

As most of us are living in a social world, we do, from time to time, have to deal with both these aspects of shame. Sometimes we might feel particularly sensitive to external shame despite generally feeling okay about ourselves. At other times we might feel really bad about ourselves even when we know others feel good about us.

External and internal shame often manifest with different focuses of attention, and distinct thoughts, feelings, and behavioural responses.

Getting to Know Our Shame

Imagine I asked you to reveal a secret to me; one that you feel very ashamed about. Let's see if we can explore that to understand what arises in us. You will find some worked examples below, and you can work through your own examples in your *Personal Practice Workbook*.

Tony

> Tony was a married man, in his 30s, two children, a nice house, a nice car, and even a cat. Everything had been going along very well until one day, during a downturn in the construction industry, he unexpectedly lost his job. The termination hit him hard. He felt stunned, lost, embarrassed and afraid. And he kept the news to himself.
>
> One thing led to another, and a month down the track, when he and I first met, he had been getting dressed every morning and heading off to work as usual, and then just trying to get through the day sitting in the park far from home, wandering the shopping centre, and going to the movies. He felt terribly ashamed about being unemployed, textured with feelings of fear and despair, and urges to hide himself and the truth of his situation from everyone, including his wife.

With respect to your own secret, let's focus on the emotions associated with having to reveal this secret and the shame it might generate. What are some of the feelings that might be there? How would you describe them? Make some notes in your *Personal Practice Workbook*.

> *What feelings are associated with Tony's shame?*
>
> I just feel so confused and lost and sad about it, and worried. I feel a kind of fear, like there's no way out. And I feel so ashamed and wish I could just hide away.

Shame can prompt a whole range of emotions. Some people will feel a lot of anxiety and fear, irritation or anger, while others might feel frozen or shut down. Either way, shame usually involves very difficult feelings that arise from the threat system and an urge to hide away.

We can also explore the concerns you might feel about what other people might think or feel about you with respect to the secret you hold, and what they might do. This is external shame. What do you think people would think, feel or do if they knew your secret?

> *What does Tony believe other people would think, feel or do if they knew his secret?*
>
> My wife would just think I'm a loser. And she'd lose any respect for me. I'm really worried that she wouldn't love me anymore, and she'd say I am no longer the man she married. She might even leave me, take the kids, and never look at me the same again.

Shame does not only arise from severe wrongdoing — sometimes it is induced by mistakes such as errors of judgment, and slips of the tongue. Or it is provoked by things that have nothing to do with our behaviours or choices, but rather characteristics that we can't change, such as our physical appearance, sexuality, or intelligence. External shame is always a focus on what others might be thinking and feeling towards us, and importantly the fear that others will view us as inadequate, inferior, unworthy and bad as a result.

Let's turn our attention to internal shame. Here, we let go a little of what others might think, and reflect on what we think and feel about ourselves. What do you think and feel about this secret that you hold? And what do you feel the urge to do? Again, make some notes in your *Personal Practice Workbook*

> ***What does Tony think, feel or do, knowing his secret?***
>
> I feel like such an idiot. I must be incompetent if I can't even keep my job. How pathetic. I'm a bad provider, and terrible husband and father. And I'm weak for not telling her about it. I just want to avoid the whole thing and try to not think about any of it.

With internal shame, any sense of other people fades into the background, and our own judgments of ourselves come into sharp focus. It's a very, very painful place to be. With internal shame the heart sinks, there is an ache of despair, and our view of ourselves is permeated by disgust. This devastatingly negative sense of ourselves as bad might be related to something we have done, but again we might experience internal shame about naturally occurring characteristics of ourselves that are no one's fault and cannot be changed.

This begs the question, what do we do when we experience shame? How do we cope with it? If we get caught up in coping behaviours that are quite maladaptive, such as using alcohol to manage anxiety, this can serve to reduce shame in the short term but perpetuate it in the longer term. So, turning again to the secret that you hold, what do you notice yourself doing to cope with the secret itself, and the shame that it causes?

> ***What does Tony do to try to cope with his experience of shame?***

> Well, I've been pretending. I get up in the morning, get dressed for work, and leave in time to catch the same train I've caught for years. But I end up at the bar and just hide there all day. And I keep secrets now, and I lie. I'd really do anything to keep this secret hidden.

Commonly, shame is managed through avoidance, escape, withdrawing, hiding, keeping secrets and/or telling lies. Remember the bodily response to shame? Slumped shoulders, bowed head, hands covering the face. This illuminates so clearly how we just want to disappear, curl up under the covers, or crawl under a rock; anything to avoid the experience and agony of shame.

Active Shaming and Memories of Being Shamed

We have explored external and internal shame as processes in the mind of the self. However, it is also true that we can experience active shaming from others, both historically and now, and this can leave its mark.

Experiences of being shamed early in life, especially as children or adolescents, have the effect of activating the threat system. Children and young people who experience a threatened social self and active shaming begin to perceive themselves as vulnerable, defective, weak or unworthy. These moments can plant seeds of shame which grow and spread into many aspects of adult life. Furthermore, this early shaming results in a child developing a view that others are critical, judgmental, unavailable and dangerous.

Memories of shame experiences can also increase the risk of experiencing external and/or internal shame in later life, as well other negative emotions, such as depression and anxiety. These shame memories lead to very negative beliefs about receiving care, compassion and love from oneself or others. We spoke before about fears of compassion, and these early experiences of shame can serve as the origin of these fears. Shame memories often foreshadow later fears of receiving compassion from others, as well as fears of self-compassion.

Shame experiences early in life may also inhibit the development of the soothing-affiliative system, and therefore one's ability to down-regulate threat and negative emotions through feeling safe and secure with others, and through the flows of compassion. When we experience active shaming, especially early in life, then we find it much more difficult to soothe ourselves or to be soothed by others.

Shame experiences can occur throughout one's life. Still, some of our most significant and potent shaming experiences happen at a young age when we are criticised or rejected by our parents. But other family members, friends, peers, teachers, coaches and many other notable people can also be a source of shaming through criticism, judgment, contempt, disdain, rejection and abuse.

Shame memories often have properties similar to trauma such as flashbacks or images of the shaming being re-experienced, urges to avoid thoughts, hyperarousal, being startled easily and having trouble with feeling safe and secure. Shame memories can also become embedded in one's self-identity, structuring the life narrative and forming a reference point to give meaning to other events. In other words, we start to define ourselves by these shaming experiences and see later circumstances and experiences through the lens of shame.

Joseph

> When Joseph first came to see me, he was distraught. He had recently separated from his wife who had demanded he leave on the basis of very large gambling debts. She was furious at him and expressed contempt for what she said were his failures as a husband, father and provider. He had moved to a cheap apartment with no furniture except a mattress on the floor and a few kitchen essentials. He was at his lowest.
>
> Almost immediately I noticed that his language was littered with severe self-criticism: 'I'm a terrible father…I'm such a bad person…I've always been a pathetic failure…Nothing I have ever done has ever been good enough. Even as a kid, I've always been stupid and weak, one big disappointment and failure.' Mixed in with all he was saying were tendrils of deep shame; ones that seemed to relate to experiences in his past.
>
> As we explored these tendrils, Joseph described his early life experiences of shame. His father, a Navy man, had been angry, aggressive and violent. Joseph's mother had been struggling with her own mental health issues, possibly exacerbated by his father's conduct, and though physically present, she was emotionally absent and neglectful. But truly what hurt Joseph the most was his father's severe shaming remarks.

'You're stupid…you're weak…man up for once…toughen up…you can't do anything right…' over and over again. Echoes of his father repeated in his mind even 30 years later, traumatising him repeatedly, and leading him to believe that these remarks defined him. He found these shame memories painfully difficult to shake. And so, in fear of others judgment and rejection as well as disgust in himself, he gambled, avoiding responsibility, hiding from reality, and escaping from pain.

How Dare You Treat Me This Way!

Not every response to shaming is anxiety, submission or an urge to hide. Sometimes, when a person is shamed by others, their reaction is anger and rage. For example, if someone puts us down or criticises us unfairly, then we can feel offended and angry. Think of classic football stadium violence which begins with one fan shaming another from the opposite team; the fan who's being shamed responds with aggression which triggers a violent response from people nearby.

This response is related to shame and is much more likely to trigger anger, rage and attack. This is *humiliation*.

Humiliation is similar to external shame, in that we are focused on the thoughts and feelings of another person; however, it is different because of the different emotions and behavioural responses it triggers. Rather than feeling anxiety, sadness or a desire to hide away, the reaction is anger and a desire to attack. 'How dare they! I'll show them!!'

Can you recall any examples of situations where you experienced a feeling of humiliation, rather than shame? Spend a few minutes reflecting on your experience of humiliation and write notes in the space provided in your *Personal Practice Workbook*.

Maybe someone was rude to you at work, or at a party? Maybe someone at home said or did something that seemed unfair to you? Humiliation might also relate to situations where people were simply being rude to you.

Humiliation, where we are made to feel stupid or embarrassed by someone else, can be problematic. Sometimes we go ahead and express the anger we feel, and lash out aggressively at the person who has humiliated us. But anger is actually very difficult to express, and often people will be fearful of expressing it. If you think about any examples of humiliation, what do you notice about being able to express your anger constructively? Were you reluctant to express that anger? What might it be that would stop you from expressing anger when someone treats you rudely or unfairly?

This is where it gets pretty complicated. Imagine you're in that same situation where you have been confronted with a rude or unfair comment or criticism that you feel is unjustified. You feel humiliated, which is a close cousin of shame, but this is different because it triggers anger and an urge to attack. But then you don't or can't express that anger because, you guessed it, shame kicks in.

We often feel ashamed of our anger. Some people don't, of course, and express it quite freely — they are far more likely to be ashamed of their sadness. But lots of people feel ashamed by their anger and frightened about what others would think of them if they allow themselves to express it. Often this anger relates to shame memories. If a child has been shamed by a parent for feeling or expressing anger, then that memory influences the way they feel about anger later.

Ann

> When Ann was a child she was fiercely criticised whenever she expressed anger. She recalled how her mother would look at her with contempt and say, 'You disgusting girl! Go to your room.' And that's where she would sit for long periods, alone and ashamed.

> By the time Ann and I were working together she was a 52-year-old married woman with young adult children. She worked full-time and looked after her ageing mother. Unfortunately, her husband, who by all reports was very unhappy in his life, was often rude and disdainful towards her and treated her quite unfairly. However, as much as this upset and angered Ann, she found it very difficult to feel and express this anger. Instead, she tried hard to suppress those feelings and was very passive in the relationship and very depressed.

> For Ann, anger had become paired with internal shame, and to express anger still meant she was a 'disgusting girl'.

Do you find you are hyper-sensitive to humiliation, and frequently respond with anger? Perhaps people around you seem to say and do things that offend you and retaliating is your habitual response?

Sometimes anger can be the easiest emotion to express. What else do you think might be there? What other feelings, behind the anger? Why do you think that anger and aggression are so readily expressed by you in these situations?

It's complicated! But unravelling all these strands of emotion and our different responses really does help us to identify the core components of how we are feeling. Once we know the components of our reaction, then we can approach each of them in a compassionate way.

One such emotion behind anger might be sadness. Perhaps a child grew up expressing sadness, only to be told by a parent or caregiver to 'man up', or 'stop crying' and the only way they were able to make sense of this was to get angry, which was then praised.

Ronsley

> Ronsley was a very successful corporate lawyer. He was known around town as 'Rampage', a nickname about which he was mostly proud. However, he was having some trouble with anger at work, especially as the pressure mounted in a big case, and his explosiveness had recently led to poorer outcomes in court.
>
> Ronsley was very closed to begin with. He was reluctant to express any emotion, especially more vulnerable ones. I asked him about this and he recounted the story of a childhood in which his father would belittle him when he cried or felt hurt. The more the father belittled him, the more he cried. He remembered one day when he randomly lashed out at his father, who said, 'Whoa ho! That's a good one. Let's see a bit of that fire in the belly.'
>
> Ronsley never forgot this lesson. *Anger is good; sadness is bad.* Anger became his default emotion and he didn't let himself feel sad ever again.

There are two basic responses to threat, and they apply to shaming experiences too. Basically, we either fight or flee.

Often, shame looks like the flight response, with a sense of inadequacy and inferiority resulting in submission, withdrawing and hiding. But often, too, it can look like the fight response, which is what happens in humiliation, with a sense of offence that provokes anger, aggression and attack. Shame and humiliation are powerful, but different, responses to self-conscious or social threats.

But I Feel Bad About What I Did

One important clarification about shame is to understand the difference between shame and another self-conscious emotion: *guilt*.

Often these two terms get confused, are used interchangeably, or are written as a pigeon pair, such as 'I feel shame and guilt'. But they are actually quite different and even arise out of different emotional systems.

As we know, shame arises out of the threat system, in that it is related to social threats. We want to be liked, valued and accepted, and need to feel a sense of belonging and position in the group. One of our greatest fears is to be judged as inadequate, inferior, unworthy and a bad person, and thereby be abandoned, rejected, or cast out of the group.

Guilt, on the other hand, is thought to arise out of the caring system. We definitely want to avoid harming those we care for and feeling guilty is a signal regarding harm avoidance and repairing any harm we might have caused. We feel guilty about doing something that damages someone we care about, but the caring motivation extends beyond our immediate family — we can also feel guilty about causing harm to other people as well.

Not only do shame and guilt arise out of separate systems; they are also quite different phenomena in and of themselves. Michael Lewis, in his 1997 book *Shame: The Exposed Self* distinguished them this way. The guilty self believes 'I have *done* something bad', while the shamed self believes 'I *am* bad.'

Guilt relates to having done something — or failed to act — in a way that causes harm that we feel regret and anguish about. It's not the same as feeling concerned about what others might think or trying to defend against the social threat of rejection — that is shame. It is our own awareness of having done something bad, and feeling regret, or sorrow, as well as remorse. It's not focused on our whole self, but rather our specific conduct.

Guilt is also an important motivator; it is usually accompanied by a wish to repair the damage we have done. So, while our conduct may have been harmful, the feeling of guilt actually motivates a return to being helpful. As such, guilt can be aligned with compassion, in that compassion is a motivation to be helpful rather than harmful.

It's easy to cause harm. Sometimes it's quite accidental, or due to thoughtlessness or carelessness and does not necessarily imply malicious intent. At other times, of course, we can harm others quite purposely, out of competition, division, jealousy or hate. However, guilt is a very important mechanism in all of these instances as it motivates us to repair the injury we have inflicted.

Shame is much more focused on the whole self, whereas guilt is more focused on specific behaviours that have caused harm. If we can accept guilt, not struggle with it too much, and tolerate the difficult pangs of sadness and regret, then it really can motivate us to repair harm, behave morally, and act in more caring ways!

External Shame, Internal Shame, Humiliation or Guilt?

Differentiating between these self-conscious emotions is useful because the approach we take to alleviate these feelings is different for each one.

- If we are experiencing external shame, then we try to take steps to re-connect with others, creating a sense of security and safeness in our relationships with them.

- For internal shame, we must work with the internal relationship of self-to-self, especially trying to manage self-criticism, and especially if it's shame-based, self-hating self-criticism.

- Repairing humiliation is different again, as the focus is understanding the role of anger in particular, and whether it is a defence against deeper shame or a different kind of outrage. Then we must find a way of tempering and letting go of the anger.

- And for guilt, we must ensure that it doesn't become shame, focused on the whole person, and instead take responsibility for our specific actions where it is warranted and take action to repair the harm we have caused where we can.

Let's have a look at an example from everyday life. Suppose that while backing out of your carpark at the shopping mall you run into another person's parked car. You may have even done this, or known someone who has. In that moment we can experience a rush of self-conscious emotion: external shame, internal shame, humiliation or guilt. Notice how these different emotions could all be possible responses in this situation:

External Shame You feel anxious, self-conscious, worried about what others might think, worried that others will blame you, judge you, see you as a fool. Your focus is on the minds of others and what they might be thinking and feeling about you.

Internal Shame You feel anxious, but also your heart sinks, and sadness creeps in. You start to blame, criticise or attack yourself as a fool. Your focus is on your whole self and how this is just typical of you. You are a careless person.

Humiliation You feel angry, outraged by the owner of the other car not parking straight. You start blaming them and focus on the unfairness. You're angry that others will unfairly blame you. You feel angry and blame others for various reasons.

Guilt You feel sadness, regret, and anxiety, for your actions and the harm you have caused. You didn't want to damage another person's property. You focus on the other person's car and the damage. You want to make amends, so you leave a note.

The Multiplicity of Self-Conscious Emotions

Earlier, we explored multiplicity from the point of view of Angry Self, Anxious Self and Sad Self. You reflected on a recent difficult situation which produced a range of strong emotions.

A similar process of differentiation is useful with self-conscious emotions as well, given many body and brain patterns can be present at any given time. It's easy to see why we get overwhelmed when we can feel external and internal shame, humiliation, and guilt, all at the same time!

Spend some time reflecting now on the point of view of your self-conscious emotions. If you like, you can write your thoughts and reflections in your *Personal Practice Workbook*.

Returning to that difficult situation, imagine that part of your experience was external shame — that others saw you as inadequate, inferior, unworthy or bad. Where would your focus of attention be? What kinds of feelings might you have? What sorts of thoughts might you have?

Now, imagine that another element involved internal shame, where you saw yourself as inadequate, inferior, unworthy, and bad. Where would your focus of attention be? What kinds of feelings might be part of this shame? What sorts of thoughts might you have?

Perhaps another component was humiliation. Imagine that part of this difficult situation was to experience humiliation and anger. Where was your attention? What kinds of feelings might have been part of this humiliation? What sorts of thoughts might you have had?

Finally, imagine that this experience also involved guilt, the sense that you had done something wrong or bad, and caused harm to another. Where would your focus of attention be? What kinds of feelings might be part of this guilt? What sorts of thoughts might you have?

It's really very complex; lots of moving parts can be present at once, working with and against each other and so conflict can arise between self-conscious emotions. We might feel humiliation and anger because we feel like we are being treated totally unfairly, but also acutely aware that others view us as unworthy. Or we might feel guilty for our own conduct in the relationship, but we are so focused on our internal shame and what a bad person we are, that any chance of repairing the damage is blocked.

Whether it be the self which is angry, anxious, sad, vulnerable, critical, vengeful or guilty, we try to bring wisdom to understand how our separate selves are functioning and what they need. Compassion does not involve ascending to a place of comfort, pleasure or happiness, but descending into the tough stuff, the agony of self-criticism, shame, humiliation and guilt…the suffering.

Time to bring the Compassionate Self to self-conscious emotion.

Bringing the Compassionate Self to Self-Conscious Emotion

One of my favourite lines from a song is from *Nature Boy*, written by Eden Ahbez and first recorded by Nat King Cole in 1948. As the song goes, 'The greatest thing you'll ever learn, is just to love and be loved in return.' I would say this is absolutely true. We are social animals who have survived because of affiliation, cooperation, and mutual care. To this day, humans simply want to love and be loved.

This is why self-conscious emotions are so painful. External shame means 'No one loves me,' internal shame means 'I don't even love me,' humiliation means 'How dare you not love me?' and guilt means 'I should love you, but I'm harming you.'

So, We Activate the Compassionate Self

Once again, find a comfortable position, either seated or standing and gently bring your body into a compassionate posture. Move your back into an upright position, with your shoulders back, chest open, head facing forwards, and with your feet flat on the floor, arms and legs uncrossed, and hands resting in your lap.

Now, start to take a few soothing breaths, bringing a soothing rhythm to your breathing. Start to slightly slow and deepen your natural breath, and lengthen the rhythm, perhaps breathing in for a count of five, and breathing out for a count of five.

Start to notice any tension or uneasiness that might be there in your body, and see if you can gradually let go of that tension.

Create a friendly facial expression. Try relaxing your facial muscles, softening your brow, relaxing your jaw, and perhaps bring a slight smile to your face.

Perhaps say silently to yourself, and with a friendly voice, in the next out-breath 'body slowing down' and in the next out-breath 'mind slowing down.' Notice how the body responds to the breathing, with a rhythm that is soothing and calming you.

Try to imagine once again what it would be like to have the qualities of compassion. Imagine what you would feel, think, and experience if you were a deeply compassionate person who had already succeeded in developing these qualities. Like an actor getting into a role or character, use your imagination to create an idea of yourself at your compassionate best, and imagine that you already have these qualities.

Now, start to imagine your Compassionate Self, that part of you that is wise, strong, and courageous.

You have a deep wisdom about the nature of life itself, that life can involve a lot of suffering, and that so many of our problems can be rooted in things that have been beyond our control. If you think about it, none of us chose the genes that we have, or the bodies that we have, or our human brain, and we didn't even choose the kind of life we have lived; and this too is not our fault.

And notice how your body and its posture, as well as your soothing breath, help to ground you, like a mountain, giving you strength and courage. Really feel that grounding in the body as you continue the soothing breathing pattern. You know that life can be difficult, and you also know that you possess the strength and courage to persist, cope and thrive.

And the Compassionate Self has a deep commitment to address suffering where ever you can, rather than turning away or avoiding, and finding the best way to be helpful. Sometimes it's not obvious and we have to learn and practice, seeking just what would be most helpful, in a curious, friendly way. The compassionate voice is a friendly voice and a helpful voice because you recognise that life is difficult.

Try to mindfully, gently and playfully imagine that you have this deep wisdom, strength, courage, and great commitment to be this type of strong, calm person with kindness and desire to be helpful. Notice how you feel when you imagine yourself like this; when you imagine having these qualities in you.

Next, consider the perspective of your Compassionate Self. What are the greatest wishes your Compassionate Self has for you? What aspirations does the Compassionate Self have for you? What would it like you to achieve out of genuine care for your well-being?

Approaching the Self-Conscious Emotions

Now let's see what the Compassionate Self's perspective might be on these self-conscious emotions, and how it might be helpful. Your thoughts and reflections of the following exercise can be recorded in your *Personal Practice Workbook*.

What does your Compassionate Self make of your feelings of external shame? External shame comes from a belief that others view you as a bad person. What does your Compassionate Self think about your external shame? How would you like to try to help alleviate the external shame?

Describe your external shame from the perspective of the Compassionate Self, and what you would like to do or say in response.

Once again, from the perspective of the Compassionate Self, what do you make of your internal shame? This is your shame-based self-criticism, sometimes self-hating, viewing yourself as a bad person. What does your Compassionate Self think about it? How would you like to help alleviate the internal shame?

Describe your internal shame from the perspective of the Compassionate Self, and what you would like to do or say to help.

What does your Compassionate Self make of your feelings of humiliation and anger, the part of you that feels you've been treated unfairly or wronged by others? What does your Compassionate Self think about your feelings of humiliation and anger? How would you like to help alleviate these emotions?

Describe your humiliation and anger from the perspective of the Compassionate Self, and what you would like to do or say to help.

Finally, what does your Compassionate Self make of your feelings of guilt? A part of you might see the harm your actions have caused and feel regret, as well as an urge to repair the damage. What does your Compassionate Self think about your feelings of guilt? How would you like to help alleviate it?

Describe your guilt from the perspective of the Compassionate Self, and what you would like to do or say to help.

We have multiples selves: different parts, modes, versions of ourselves that arise depending on the context, situation and, of course, our own life experiences. And the multiples interact, working together in one moment, and then in conflict with each other in the next, supercharging their complexity and their impact.

The Compassionate Self enters the fray with wisdom, strength and courage, and commitment to being helpful rather than harmful. The Compassionate Self understands the self-conscious emotions, their function and purpose, and the way they can hurt. It knows that none of this is our fault, but is able to guide us towards managing these multiple selves so that we suffer less.

The Compassionate Self feels deeply moved by our painful self-conscious emotions; this is really tough stuff. And so we remember to breathe, bring a gentle smile to our face, create a grounded sensation in our bodies, and approach the self-conscious emotions with compassionate intention to alleviate suffering.

Always remember: validation, reassurance, encouragement.

Three Pearls

Chapter 9 has explored one of the tougher emotions: shame. Having said that, shame is also common, and most of us have had shame experiences in our lives. Most of us also have tricky memories of those experiences. But there are things we can do, not least bringing compassion to our shame. Write down three pearls in your *Personal Practice Workbook*, things you would like to remember, reflect upon, or put into practice about working with shame.

Chapter 10

Forgiving You, Forgiving Me and Having Healthy Relationships

What is Forgiveness, and What Isn't It?

Forgiveness can be a powerful act of compassion and self-compassion. However, people often struggle with the concept of forgiveness, as well as the practice of forgiving.

When someone else hurts us, we can feel anxious and sad, but we can also feel angry, even enraged, at the person who perpetrated the harm. We can feel a burning desire to retaliate or seek revenge. And this desire can go on and on, often unfulfilled, while the anger and rage persist. Sometimes these emotions can turn inward and become self-destructive.

*Holding onto anger is like drinking poison
and waiting for the other person to die.*

I'm not certain of the origins of this saying which is sometimes attributed to the Buddha, although it is not found in the scriptures. One very early reference is from the Buddhist scholar Buddhaghosa in his 5th-century great work Visuddhimagga. He wrote this about anger: 'By doing this you are like a man who wants to hit another and picks up a burning ember or excrement in his hand and so first burns himself or makes himself stink.'

This saying contains a lot of wisdom: ruminating on anger and rage, and nurturing a desire to seek vengeance, are toxic for the person who persists with holding onto those thoughts.

This is why we try to practice forgiveness: letting go of anger and rage and the desire for retaliation and vengeance is in our own best interests, for our bodies and our brains. Forgiveness is a way to enact compassion, and be helpful, rather than harmful, to ourselves and others.

The first step with forgiveness is to connect again with what it is to be human and have a complex human brain, and all the chaos and craziness that comes along with it. We know people do bad things. They can be careless, callous or cruel. That is a part of how we have evolved to be. Recognising that as a first step can help with forgiveness.

The second step is to understand that forgiveness is not actually something we necessarily do for others. Forgiveness is really an act of self-compassion, something we do for ourselves. By forgiving others, we can temper the anger and rage, and let go of feelings of retaliation or vengeance, all for the sake of our own wellbeing.

Let's be clear. Forgiveness does not mean we condone the conduct or accept the unwanted conduct, and it certainly does not indicate we are giving permission for poor behaviour to occur again.

Forgiveness might not even involve an apology from the other person. If we hold on too tightly to the notion that the person who harmed us should apologise first, then we will continue to be trapped in anger and rage. Learning to forgive without an apology can be liberating!

Forgiveness also does not mean that you have to reunite with the person who hurt you. You may wish to reconcile, or you may not, but you may decide that it is safer to stay away from them. Sometimes the person who hurt you or whom you wish to forgive has died or left your life, and yet we still want to be able to forgive them.

And forgiveness is not forgetting what the other person did or pretending it didn't happen. We can forgive others while remembering what they did and endeavouring to prevent them from harming us again. It's unrealistic to think you will never be hurt again, but we do learn from experience and can put in place mechanisms and boundaries that reduce its likelihood.

Consider your point of view on forgiveness. Spend five minutes working through the following questions and writing your thoughts and reflections in your *Personal Practice Workbook*.

- What do you think some of the benefits of forgiveness are for you?
- What thoughts or attitudes do you feel could inhibit your forgiveness, make you feel reluctant to forgive, or generally get in your way?
- What might be some things that might help you to be forgiving towards others?
- How do you think the Compassionate Self might be able to help you with forgiveness?

Empathy as a Part of Forgiveness

When another person has hurt or harmed us, it's important to remember they are just like us; they have all of the same positive and negative traits, and they have their own life experiences which have shaped them. As part of the process of forgiving, we practice empathy so we can understand another person's perspective and what might be going on beneath the surface for them. One common saying is, 'Hurt people hurt people,' and frequently, when we consider what is going on beneath the surface for the person who hurt us, we realise that they, too, are suffering.

Empathy is a competency of compassion, and it is also a competency of forgiveness. It involves *affective empathy*, the ability to resonate with the feelings of another, and *cognitive empathy*, the ability to understand the other's perspective. This means we bring our conscious attention to the mind of the other person, their motives, urges, and desires, and understand what might be driving their patterns of behaviour. This gives us clues about how we might engage with them, behave with them, and ultimately forgive them.

Remember, empathy is different from sympathy. Empathy is being able to feel and understand the feelings and meanings of the *other person;* sympathy is feeling our own response to another person's suffering. With empathy, we are focused on understanding the feelings of the other person and how those feelings originate and exist within them.

As part of forgiveness, we want to have empathy not only for the other person but also for ourselves. Self-empathy is important; we need to understand ourselves, our feelings and meanings across our multiple selves. When we are beginning the process of forgiving another person, we also turn our empathic attunement towards ourselves, understanding the many layers of responses that we may be having.

Compassion for Others, Compassion for Self

Forgiveness is a unique combination of compassion for others and compassion for ourselves. We are focused particularly on those two flows. As such, we are activating the Compassionate Self to forgive in order to potentially be helpful to all involved. If you notice yourself baulking when you read that statement, that's quite natural. You have a tricky brain! It's not easy to let go of the anger and the desire for retaliation or revenge.

Being compassionate towards another person, and forgiving them, is most difficult when it is someone:

- who is very different from us.
- who holds different values, values that we disagree with or perhaps abhor.
- with whom we are in disagreement, dispute or conflict.
- who has done something harmful or hurtful towards us, or those we care about.

So, we try to connect again with the wisdom that we all have complex brains, and accept we all get caught in loops. It is not our fault that we have genes we did not choose or life circumstances and experiences, but it is our responsibility to manage ourselves. And when we are nominating our Compassionate Self to be a greater part of who we are, we need to understand that forgiveness is not easy, but it is an opportunity for a better future. For those who are most difficult to forgive, there still needs to be changes, consequences or boundaries, but, wherever possible, without anger, hatred or vengeance.

Compassion in the case of forgiveness is about being true to ourselves and our principles, and giving the other person the best opportunity to also be at their compassionate best, keeping in mind that we can never control how someone else responds, speaks or behaves.

Compassion in me can be met with compassion in you.

And forgiveness is all about self-compassion too — may I be helpful, rather than harmful, to *myself* and others. Forgiveness is a wonderful example of how self-compassion is not necessarily an easier option. It's like starting physical exercise, which can at first be unpleasant and even punishing, but we do it because we know that, in the end, it's good for us.

Softening anger and letting go of a desire for retaliation and vengeance can be very difficult. It can even seem nonsensical. *Why on earth would I forgive this person who has hurt me so much?* Notice the threat system activation implied in that statement? But a self-compassionate motivation understands that forgiveness is still the best way to be helpful, rather than harmful, to ourselves, and truly is in direct service of our own wellbeing.

Forgiveness is an exquisite combination of compassion for others and compassion for yourself.

May I Begin to Forgive

Forgiveness often requires concerted efforts and repeated attempts; we can't forgive people in one go. We have to be gentle with ourselves, not expect too much too quickly, and give the experience a chance to settle in. One danger is that we use the anger to try to make ourselves forgive, such as, 'That bastard, I'll forgive him. That'll show him!!' It sounds strange, but sometimes we feel driven to forgive by our desire to retaliate. The threat system is still running the show!

So we bring it back to the body and settle ourselves into a compassionate posture. By now, you might be finding this much more familiar. The back is straight; the shoulders are back, the chest is open, arms relaxed, hands in the lap, feet flat on the floor. A calm mind thinks differently, so slow down the breath to create a soothing rhythm, and on the out-breath we say silently to ourselves, in a friendly voice, 'body slowing down,' and then 'mind slowing down'.

Start to activate your Compassionate Self, that part of you that has wisdom and understanding, strength, courage, dignity and authority, and a commitment to be helpful. Set an intention to set yourself free, to let go, and to soften the anger and rage that is in danger of getting in the way of you truly flourishing. Also, see if you can set a benevolent intention towards others, that they will live peaceful, safe, and happy lives, free of suffering, and with compassion in their own hearts.

Now bring to mind a person who has hurt you, and whom you are willing to begin to forgive. Imagine the presence of that person in this moment and consider, as best you can, that person's perspective: their thoughts, feelings, needs and intentions. And consider their problematic human brain with all its tradeoffs and its inherent suffering.

Recall the moment you felt hurt by them. And if you are comfortable to begin the process of moving towards forgiving that person, say to yourself the following:

> May I begin to forgive this person for what they did, intentionally or unintentionally, to hurt me in some way.
>
> May I acknowledge the pain that this person has caused me, and soften and soothe my anger, to set myself free and move on.
>
> May I commit, wherever possible, to not being hurt like this again, by this person or anybody else, to the best of my abilities.

Nadia

> Marital breakdown and the breakdown of other types of close relationships can be excruciating, and there can be hurtful actions taken by both parties.

Nadia's marriage had ended when both she and her husband had affairs. The couple had three young children, they both worked and tried to look after the kids together, but the love had disappeared from their relationship some years before. Unbeknownst to each other, they had begun affairs with third parties in uncannily similar circumstances and at about the same time. When they discovered what had been happening, they parted ways. It was tough, an unhappy time, but they separated relatively amicably.

Unfortunately, the hurt for Nadia only amplified as time went on. Her relationship with her affair partner didn't work out, and not long after her marital separation, this other relationship came to an abrupt end. Her ex-husband, on the other hand, continued his relationship with his affair partner, who after a year or so he married, and they had another child together. In the three years that had passed since separation, Nadia hadn't re-partnered and felt very lonely, hurt and angry.

Nadia projected her anger towards her ex-husband. She was vicious in the things she said about him, and the things she said to him, which affected him to a certain extent, however most of the time he carried on seemingly happily in his new life. Nadia and I talked long and hard about this anger, where the anger was coming from, the apparent function of this anger, and the effects the anger was really having for her.

It quickly became clear that the main consequence of the anger was ongoing harm to herself, her emotional state, and possibly even how she was as a parent to her children. It was a long road, but she decided that she couldn't do this to herself any longer. She needed to forgive her ex-husband, not so much for him as for her own sake. Gradually she got there, and it had a very positive effect. After that, she was able to turn her attention to dating again!

A Letter of Forgiveness

You may also wish to write a letter of forgiveness to the person who has hurt you. This does not mean you have to send it — the purpose of the letter is to honestly express how you feel, and work through a process of forgiveness. The writing, not the delivery, is the powerful aspect of this exercise.

Your letter can say anything you need to say — just remember it is coming from a place of compassion for others and yourself. You might include a description of how this person hurt you, a statement of forgiveness for the hurt this caused, an intention to be free of the anger or desire for vengeance, and a plan to set appropriate boundaries to ensure you won't be hurt like this again.

Here is an example of a letter of forgiveness another client of mine wrote to her ex-boyfriend. For many years, she had felt deeply hurt and bitterly angry about how her ex-boyfriend had separated from her. Even after a decade had passed, she felt unable to move on with her life or open herself up to a new relationship; the separation had affected her life so much that she had become terribly isolated and lonely. Her willingness to begin to forgive her ex-boyfriend was a vitally important turning point for her to start to live her life more fully.

> A Letter of Forgiveness
>
> Dear Haru
>
> I am writing this letter to let you know how much you have hurt me, and also to forgive you for what you did. When I came home and realised that you had packed all your things and left, I felt so much pain that I collapsed on the floor. Your choice to leave like that, after promising that you loved me and wanted to marry me, hurt so deeply and left me feeling so small and alone. And I have carried so much painful anger with me for so long that my life has been completely stifled.
>
> I realise that what you did was to a large extent motivated by fear and self-protection. But it really hurt me. Nevertheless, I forgive you for what you did. I am willing now to let go of my anger and to move on from this experience. I'm going to do my best to not let anyone hurt me like this again, however, I am also not going to let my experience with you cause me to be so fearful of being hurt again that I can't ever have another relationship.
>
> From now on, I'm going to do my best to feel safe and connected with others.
>
> From Hana

Perhaps you could try to write a letter of forgiveness to someone who has hurt you. You can always start with someone whose conduct towards you was at the moderate end of the spectrum; gently work your way up to more challenging people as you practice writing and become more

When the Person We Need to Forgive is Ourselves

Sometimes, we might be the one who, through carelessness, callousness, or cruelty, has caused hurt or harm, and the reality of own behaviour can be very difficult to confront. We often find all sorts of ways to justify or excuse our own conduct.

'It was an accident,' or 'She deserved it,' or 'He asked for it.'

When we truly connect with the Compassionate Self, we begin to find the strength and courage to approach our own harmful conduct, perhaps make amends, but also to find self-forgiveness.

Frank

> I once worked with a combat veteran who had carried fifty years of remorse over his involvement in a firefight. The conflict had taken place at night among some trees; it was a chaotic scene. The enemy was all around, but so were his own men, and Frank was doing his best by firing into the surrounding darkness. He didn't know who he might have hit, but he had never been able to forgive himself for the possibility it might have been one of his own.
>
> Gradually as we worked together, he began to consider the situation from the wisdom of his Compassionate Self. He knew and understood that he was 18 years old at the time, his threat system was peaking, and his brain was doing its absolute best to keep him alive. With strength and courage, he used imagery to approach his younger self, and offered himself forgiveness for the harm he may have caused, quite unwittingly, in a state of incomparable terror. He also vowed to not cause this kind of harm, or other harm, again in his life.
>
> It was a poignant moment of emancipation from the shackles of guilt, regret and anger that he had for so long directed at himself.

This might also be something you could try. Many of the practices described above regarding forgiving others can apply to self-forgiveness. Finding a compassionate position, and taking deep and soothing breaths, start to activate your Compassionate Self, your wisdom, strength and courage, and commitment to be helpful. Set your intention to let go of guilt and regret, or any anger you may feel towards yourself. Activate a compassionate motivation towards yourself, and your wish to be free from suffering.

Bring to mind a moment or scenario where you have hurt someone else. Create an image of yourself in that situation and of the other person. Again, take your time. Consider, if you can, the perspective of that person who you hurt, their thoughts, feelings, and needs. And consider the situation from your own perspective in that situation, understanding your own thoughts, feelings, needs, intentions, desires, motivations, urges, and so on. Remember, you have a human brain, with all its tradeoffs, its good and not so good bits, and its suffering. If it feels right to begin to forgive yourself, consider, and say to yourself, the following:

> May I begin to forgive myself for what I did, intentionally or unintentionally, to cause this other person pain in some way.
>
> May I acknowledge the hurt that I have caused them, and soften and soothe my regret and anger, to set myself free and move on.
>
> May I commit, where ever possible, to not cause hurt like this again, to this person or anybody else, to the best of my abilities.

Setting Boundaries with Compassionate Assertiveness

There are many ways in which a compassionate motivation can be practised, and one such way relates to being able to understand and express your own wants and needs through compassionate assertiveness.

Much has been written about assertiveness, but from the point of view of the Compassionate Self, assertiveness involves a number of elements to consider. We start by working towards being aware of ourselves and others in any given situation. We try to bring awareness and understanding to the different perspectives of all those involved, especially around wants and needs, as well as any feelings of dissatisfaction, disappointment or distress. We recognise that those involved may have made interpretations of one another, and feel hurt by those interpretations, rather than what was intended. There is a lot of wisdom in compassionate assertiveness.

And there is strength and courage! As part of compassionate assertiveness, we acknowledge and even admit that we have contributed to the difficult situation without feeling too defensive or sensitive. We try to accept that we might have different perspectives from others and that this does not mean we are being attacked or derided. Having a separate and distinct view from another person does not make anyone wrong. We want to be able to clearly state our own perspective or position, and calmly hear the perspective of the other people involved. We recognise that we are different, and we make every effort to take this into account as we navigate the situation.

Empathy plays a vital role in compassionate assertiveness. We stay committed to being genuinely empathic towards other people involved, most notably by really listening.

In compassionate assertiveness we are listening to understand, rather than listening to respond

This is an important difference. The purpose of listening is to enhance our understanding of the other person. Self-empathy has the same objective; we are trying to have a good understanding of ourselves, as well as the minds of others.

Out of compassionate assertiveness can also come good boundaries. In terms of the conduct of the other people involved, be clear about what you feel is okay, and what you feel is not okay.

Everyone needs healthy boundaries and being able to be clear about what the boundary is, and then also clearly expressing that, is key to compassionate assertiveness. Equally, we have to set boundaries for ourselves. Our own conduct might stray across the line between what's okay and what's not okay, and some of our behaviours might be perpetuating the problematic conduct of others. So, in compassionate assertiveness, we are also willing and able to set boundaries for ourselves.

Finally, compassionate assertiveness involves a positive twist. We try to nurture a positive exchange through praising, affirming, complementing and appreciating the other person. We will look into appreciation, but let's dive a bit further into compassionate assertiveness first.

Aggression, submission, or assertion?

Imagine you are with a friend, and they ask to borrow money that you really don't have to lend them. There are many ways in which you could respond.

One option might fall into an aggressive response, where you try to win at all costs; another might be to fall into a submissive response, where you forfeit all too easily. Both these responses are likely to involve a combination of threat and drive, or more specifically, a sense of competition.

Compassionate assertiveness is fundamentally linked with a different motivational system, namely the soothing-affiliative system via social awareness, understanding and intention, and having primarily a compassionate motivation. The goal here is not about winning or losing, or competing, but rather finding a way to a mutually helpful and beneficial outcome.

Returning to the example of the friend who has asked to borrow money, consider the following worked example of aggressive, submissive and compassionately assertive responses, and reflect on your own likely responses in this sort of situation. Write your thoughts in your *Personal Practice Workbook*.

Aggressiveness	[Shouting] How dare you! What sort of a friend are you? You can't manage your own finances! I wouldn't lend you a dollar!
Submissiveness	[Anxiously] Oh, of course, of course. How much do you need, I have plenty. Just get it back to me whenever you can.
Compassionate Assertiveness	[Friendly, respectful, clear] I'm so sorry. I can see that you are struggling with finances at the moment. I would like to help ... only my own finances are complex at the moment. Is there any other way I could help out?

Compassionate assertiveness: kind, warm, friendly, wise, strong, clear, honest, and firm

Let's Assert!

See if you can bring to mind a common scenario when you would have trouble asking for what you need, or setting a clear boundary. Perhaps it's so difficult that you are much more likely to simply avoid asking. You might think of a situation with a specific person, or a recurring situation where you have trouble saying no. It might be at home or work, with family, friends or colleagues. If you like, use your *Personal Practice Workbook* to make some notes about the situation you are bringing to mind, and then work through the rest of this exercise.

Now activate your Compassionate Self. Settle in, with a posture that is upright but relaxed. Open up the chest and the diaphragm. Gradually slow your breath, perhaps to a count of in-for-five, and out-for-five. Prompt yourself with 'body slowing down,' and then 'mind slowing down.' Ground yourself and connect with a sense of confidence.

As you reflect on this situation where you find it difficult to be assertive from the perspective of the Compassionate Self:

- What are your thoughts?
- What are your feelings?
- What are your wants and needs?
- What feels okay, and what does not feel okay?
- From the perspective of the Compassionate Self, what would you like to say, what would you like to do?
- From the perspective of the Compassionate Self, what are the boundaries that you might wish to set for yourself and others?

Expressing Appreciation

As funny as this might sound, expressing appreciation for another person can be difficult. We often experience blocks to doing so, and we can struggle with saying supportive and generous things out loud.

And yet, expressing appreciation for the characteristics or attributes of another person can have a whole range of positive effects, such as helping them to feel valued, boosting confidence, creating a closer connection, and developing a burgeoning sense of goodwill. This can also be especially helpful in future, more difficult situations that you might experience with them.

Praise can be helpful too, although praise, like punishment, is designed to influence another person's future conduct. When we praise someone, we are encouraging them to keep doing the behaviour we are praising. Compliments are like praise in that we are passing judgment on the person; it's undoubtedly a positive judgment, but a judgment nonetheless. In a way, both praise and compliments can create a power imbalance in which a person who sees themselves as superior is casting positive judgment down on the inferior person.

Appreciation, like gratitude, can be a way to elevate the other person, putting them somewhat above you. In a way, you are truly prizing the other person's characteristics and qualities. Appreciation moves away from praising conduct or complimenting more superficial aspects and moves towards the person's strength, qualities, values, and contributions. Where praise might say, 'You look lovely in that dress,' appreciation would go deeper and say, 'I really admire your grace and poise.'

If you think about expressing appreciation to a loved one, what are some of the blocks or resistances that arise? Do you notice any threat system activation? Anxiety? Self-consciousness? What comes up for you?

What about receiving appreciation? What are some of the blocks or resistances you experience if someone else expresses appreciation towards you? Do you notice any threat system activation? Self-criticism? What comes up for you?

How might you use the Compassionate Self to help with expressing or accepting appreciation?

Expressing and accepting appreciation are both great ways to gently expose yourself to positive emotions in order to become more and more comfortable with them. Again, it sounds strange, but it takes practice. The Compassionate Self can really help by creating a sense of safeness that allows us to open up to positive emotions.

What could you do to express appreciation to people in your life? What could you start with? What sorts of things could you say?

Spend five or ten minutes reflecting on giving and receiving appreciation, and write your notes in your *Personal Practice Workbook*.

Three Pearls

The Compassionate Self is also a vital part of our relationships, whether it be forgiving ourselves and others, or finding a way to be assertive and appreciative. Chapter 10 talked about compassionate forgiveness and compassionate assertiveness. Perhaps you could write three pearls in your *Personal Practice Workbook*.

Chapter 11

Practical Strategies for Deepening your Compassionate Self

Recapping the Core Principles

Suffering is part of life. That was the first line of this book, and it is still true as we approach its end. We will all experience ageing, sickness, injury, disablement and eventually death. We will also suffer when people we love go through these challenges and we are unable to protect them.

Human beings have very complex brains, that are wonderful and agonising in equal measure. We have absolutely no choice in how it works, or the particular quirks and idiosyncrasies that our brains happen to have. A lot of our suffering is already laid down the moment we are born and none of that is our fault.

Once we are born, life starts to happen. How incredible that, by random, dumb luck, we have been born at this time. Had it been 50 years earlier, our lives would be completely different. All of our socio-demographics are also completely random: gender, place of birth, family of origin, race, culture, religion, family income, education and so on.

Understanding how the brain works really helps us, as well as knowing that everything it does is due to one or other of its evolutionary functions. Then we can start to approach our mind, and become an observer of what it is doing from moment to moment, the negative and the positive.

Compassion is also an evolved motivation. It begins with the mammalian caring motivation and is magnified by uniquely human competencies of social awareness and understanding, mentalising and perspective-taking, and setting conscious intentions to be helpful.

As we endeavour to understand and manage our human brains and the trouble they can sometimes cause us, we activate compassion to allow us to *engage* with those things that are uncomfortable, disappointing, painful or upsetting. We work towards being open to suffering, and in non-judgmental ways, not causing further suffering through blaming and shaming. We start to explore those different aspects of ourselves that can cause us trouble: our multiple selves and our self-conscious emotions.

Once engaged, our compassionate motivation encourages taking *action* that attempts to alleviate or prevent the suffering, always starting by bringing it back to the body. We work hard to create the image of a compassionate other, and then the image of a Compassionate Self who serves as a guide and inspiration. We start the conversation between our multiple selves, and our self-conscious emotions, with our Compassionate Self.

As we come closer to the end of this book, consider any ways in which you may have become more compassionate towards others, and more open to receiving compassion, including from yourself. Use your *Personal Practice Workbook* to record some examples, no matter how small, of your Compassionate Self in action.

Sometimes we can experience fears, blocks or resistances to compassion. It's always useful to watch out for these inhibitors, and useful to reflect on your experience of these now. What have you noticed has inhibited your compassion towards others, being open to receiving compassion from others, or offering compassion to yourself?

From here, the practice continues! Working off the familiar adage — *may I be helpful, rather than harmful, to myself and others* — let's explore some practical strategies to deepen your practice of compassion.

Breathing with Affection

We have spoken about the value of softening and slowing the breathing as a way to activate the parasympathetic nervous system. This is a fundamental exercise in activating the Compassionate Self, however, there are other approaches to breathing that can also be useful to develop. One of these, known as affectionate breathing, is part of the Mindful Self-Compassion program developed by US researchers Dr Kristin Neff and Dr Chris Germer, and is designed to use the breath to bring affection to yourself and your experience.

Begin by allowing your body to find a comfortable position, finding a posture that's relaxed, but reasonably upright. Try to keep your back straight and gently supported, your chest open, shoulders back and relaxed, and facing forward. Bring a friendly expression to your face.

Take three, slow, easy breaths, letting go of whatever tensions you may be carrying. You may also wish to place a hand or both hands over your heart, as a small gesture of kindness, affection and physical comfort towards yourself.

Now bring your attention to your own breath. Notice the subtle physical sensations of the gentle rise and fall of your chest or the air passing softly in and out through your nostrils. Just bring a gentle curiosity to your own breath for a few minutes.

You might notice that your mind wanders away from the focus on the breath. And that's perfectly okay. Notice these thoughts, acknowledge them, smile to them, and then bring your attention back to your breath.

Now see if you can gently lean in towards your breathing, just as you might lean in towards a child who you love, with tenderness and interest. Move towards your breath with a feeling of fondness and affection. Notice how your breath sustains you, your body and mind, always there, even when you're not really aware of it.

Notice how your whole body moves as you breathe. There's a gentle rise and fall, like the movement of the calm sea. In a way, the breath is rocking you, soothing and caressing you.

Take a moment and savour the comfort you may feel in your body.

Colouring to Compassion

We have used a lot of imagery throughout this book. It's such a powerful method of cultivating a compassionate motivation and the Compassionate Self, and yet it is not necessarily easy for everyone. Some people actually find specific imagery very difficult, but can more easily imagine light or colours.

Create your compassionate posture, and start to slowly, gently imagine that you are surrounded by a beautiful, compassionate light or glow. What colours or hues would you like to see in this light? Now, imagine this energy is flowing around and within you.

As you breathe, the energy, formed of light and colour, is flowing into your lungs and throughout your whole body. The warmth of this energy is filling your lungs, your heart, your abdomen, and your arms and legs, filling your entire being with compassion. It warms you, soothes you, and fills you with compassionate intention.

This compassionate light or energy is warm, friendly and healing, helpful, and comforting. That's its function: to heal. Just like an ointment that soothes and heals a wound, this compassionate energy is there to help all parts of your body, as well as parts of your mind that may also be suffering.

Imagine your body now glowing with compassion, perhaps a bright or clear light, or a soft mist of colour, whatever feels right for you. When we activate the Compassionate Self, we can imagine ourselves glowing with compassionate light or energy. This can be very helpful and definitely worth trying to see if it is helpful to include in your practice.

Writing a Compassionate Letter to Yourself

Another way to activate the Compassionate Self is through writing. This accesses a different part of the brain than imagery, and so for those who find imagery difficult, writing can be a great alternative. Taking your thoughts out of your head and putting them on paper can be a powerful way to start to think differently or see things in alternative ways.

Let's start with a current life difficulty that you are experiencing. Perhaps it is a disagreement at home or a challenge at work. Again, nothing too major, but something that is creating some discomfort, concern or frustration. Write a brief description of this current life difficulty in your *Personal Practice Workbook*.

Next, activate your Compassionate Self through your body, and engage with your wisdom, strength and courage, and commitment. Start to write a letter to yourself *from your Compassionate Self*. And as you do, just remember a few important things:

- Express understanding, empathy and *validation* for your difficulty.
- Show genuine care, sympathy, *reassurance*, and support.
- Focus on your strengths, capabilities, and courage.
- Offer *encouragement* and support, and suggestions of anything helpful.
- Don't get too directive, advice-giving, or telling, and avoid 'shoulds' and 'oughts'.

Here is an example of a letter written by a woman I worked with to her frustrated Angry Self from her Compassionate Self.

> A Letter of Compassion
>
> Dear Jan
>
> I know you are feeling really frustrated right now. I completely understand why you might feel like this. These situations are complex. I also know you have worked really hard on becoming more aware of yourself and your feelings, and how to manage all this better. You're getting there! And you are tapping into courage, as well as the wisdom of knowing what you really need. You know that a calm mind thinks differently, so let's take a little time out, breath, slow and soothe the body and mind, and start to think about what you really need right now, what might be most helpful.
>
> Your Compassionate Self

Write a letter from your Compassionate Self about this life difficulty you are experiencing at the moment. Don't worry about spelling and punctuation. You may find certain parts of yourself chime in, such as self-conscious self. Don't worry. Just write with heartfelt authenticity, from your Compassionate Self. You can use the space provided in your *Personal Practice Workbook*.

Compassion in Your Pocket

As the old saying goes, where ever you go, you take you with you! This refers to the fact that if we try to run away from our problems, they tend to follow us. But it's also true that where ever you go, your Compassionate Self goes with you. And to make this more readily accessible, sometimes it can be useful to carry a prompt to remind us that our Compassionate Self is always there alongside us ready to help.

Using the compassionate letter you wrote, see if you can make a flashcard of compassionate words to keep in your pocket, wallet or purse. Identify three or four key thoughts or ideas that feel really helpful when you're faced with a difficult situation. The idea is that when you need it, you can refer to this flashcard and then, in a compassionate voice, offer yourself these words of wisdom, strength and support.

For example, Jan's flashcard read:

> Life is tricky;
>
> Wisdom and courage — you're getting there;
>
> Remember, a calm mind thinks differently.

What might be three or four or ideas for a flashcard that would help you keep compassion in your pocket? Maybe you could create actual flashcards that you keep in your wallet or purse. You can also write down the ideas that come to mind in your *Personal Practice Workbook*.

Another interesting option is to have a small, portable material object that you carry with you as a reminder or prompt for your Compassionate Self. I have known people to carry a small semi-precious stone that reminds them to stay grounded, or a necklace left to them by their grandmother who was a very compassionate person. The possibilities are endless! The idea is to find something that has special meaning for you and can help you stay connected to your Compassionate Self.

Mirror, Mirror

Next time you are getting dressed in the morning or brushing your teeth at night, notice what it is like to look in the mirror. Often these can be painfully analytical and critical moments of the day. 'Oh, I'm so gross,' 'Ugh, my hair looks terrible.' Some people can't even bring themselves to look due to self-criticism or even self-disgust.

What happens for you when you look in the mirror? What thoughts or feelings arise? What analytical or critical thoughts do you have when you look at yourself in the mirror?

Those moments when we look at ourselves in the mirror are also an opportunity to see ourselves differently, perhaps as others see us, with a warm, friendly and compassionate sentiment. It's not easy, because we are often the least objective, most negatively biased judges of ourselves, but others see us much more objectively and without bias.

Approaching ourselves with compassion in the mirror is a very powerful way to cultivate compassion towards ourselves, although it can be difficult. We get easily distracted by imperfections, a wish to change them, and a feeling of self-dislike or loathing. This is natural, but we want to bring compassion to the darker aspects of ourselves, and where better to do that than face-to-face with ourselves in the mirror.

How would someone else who loves me see me? What would be their focus? How would I see someone else that I love? What would be my focus? How would they approach me and how would I approach them? What would we say? Incorporating these different perspectives, how might the Compassionate Self approach this? How might the Compassionate Self find a way to be helpful, rather than harmful, in and around these painful emotions?

Next time you are at a mirror, or at a time when you feel ready to do so, first activate your Compassionate Self. Bring a friendly expression to your face, and from a place of wisdom, strength and courage, and commitment to being helpful, gently open your eyes and see your own face in all its uniqueness and beauty.

What does your Compassionate Self focus on in the face in the mirror? What discomfort, disappointment, pain, or suffering does your Compassionate Self notice in the face in the mirror?

What does the Compassionate Self see *behind* the face, behind the eyes that are looking back at you? Can the Compassionate Self see the wants and needs, the suffering?

Bring a warm friendliness to your face, and soften your eyes so that they say, 'I understand, I feel for you, I want to help you.' Offer yourself words of compassion, infused with a deep desire to be supportive and helpful. What would you whisper softly to yourself in the mirror to be helpful?

Write down your responses to the above questions in your *Personal Practice Workbook* so you can try this every day. Meet your face and those eyes in the mirror with a compassionate intention. This is a chance to persist with yourself, despite the feelings of self-consciousness, embarrassment, or reluctance. Repetition is important for creating new body and brain patterns. Keep going! You are conveying genuine and committed care.

> I look in the mirror.
>
> All I see is blemishes and flaws.
>
> I soften my brow. I smile.
>
> I see my face, my eyes.
>
> I turn my gaze to what lies behind.
>
> I see the suffering that dwells
>
> there in the darker spaces.
>
> And I say,
>
> 'I am here for you, and I always will be.'

Compassion in Daily Life

Compassion and self-compassion can gradually become increasingly part of who we are. We start by learning the ideas, concepts and theories, using our bodies, imagery, colours and other experiential practices. But if we are to embody compassion, we need to find ways to build compassionate motivation and action into our daily life.

With practice, rehearsal and repetition, we can start to make the Compassionate Self more habitually activated. Eventually, when we experience something disappointing or difficult, the Compassionate Self will arrive quite automatically to offer comfort and support.

Mei

> Mei was really struggling with a difficult form of internal shame, which was very self-destructive, and tragically caused her to damage all her relationships leaving her feeling terribly alone. She came to see me one day and was very keen to tell me about an experience she'd had during the week.
>
> Mei said she'd been really suffering from her shame and self-loathing one particular day and couldn't leave the house. She was having all sorts of very worrying, self-harming thoughts. Feeling frantic and distressed, she went into her room and lay on the bed. Just then a voice came to her mind, her own voice, and said softly, 'This is really tough. You're going through a lot. But you'll be okay; you'll get there. Just rest a moment, breathe, and then let's get up and give Jacey a call.'
>
> She was delighted to finally welcome the spontaneous voice of her Compassionate Self.

Consider how to start building compassion and self-compassion into your daily life. See if you can think of something you could do each day that would be an example of compassionate behaviour. Every compassionate action, no matter how big or small, and whether you really feel like it or not, helps shift your general state of mind and perspective little by little.

Remember the three flows of compassion:

- Compassion towards others. This can be very important to include in your life, benefitting both the person you are being compassionate towards, as well as benefitting yourself.

- Compassion towards yourself. Small acts of self-compassion can be quite life-changing!

- Receiving compassion from others. This third flow of compassion can be the most difficult for some people, but we are social animals and we need connection. A sure way to truly soothe anger, anxiety, sadness, or shame is to receive compassion from others.

Here are 99 ideas (in no order, both great and small) to continue your journey towards greater compassionate action in your daily life. Which ones seem most attractive to you?

1. Smile to a stranger in the street or say, 'Good morning.'
2. Say a sincere 'Thank you!' to a shop assistant or compliment their work.
3. Let an anxious-looking driver merge in front of you in traffic.
4. Donate to a cause you feel strongly about.
5. Teach English to a refugee or new arrival to your country.
6. Hold an elevator for someone carrying heavy bags.
7. Adopt an unwanted dog or cat.
8. Volunteer for a charity that provides for the basic needs of disadvantaged people.
9. Travel overseas to help in the construction of a school.
10. Invite someone who is in a rush to go ahead of you in line.
11. Make a meal for a family with a newborn baby and sleepless nights.
12. Read to children who are having trouble with their learning.
13. Donate clothes, toys or other items to a charity.
14. Mow a friend's lawn when they are going through a hard time.
15. Start working shifts at a soup kitchen.
16. Visit a local nursing home and play music or sing songs.
17. Call a friend you haven't seen for a while and ask how they are doing.
18. Introduce yourself to someone new at work or at school.
19. Become a foster parent or contribute to supporting foster families.
20. Volunteer to support children who are involved in the court system.
21. Work with a nature care group or volunteer in animal rescue.
22. Devote more time to elderly relatives and listen to their old stories.
23. Write an article that might touch someone else and inspire them with your story.
24. Give your unused musical instruments to a local school.
25. Join a community organisation that helps local people in need.
26. Ask someone, 'Are you okay?' and then wholeheartedly give attention to their response.

27. Stop and take time to talk to someone who perhaps appears to be living on the streets.
28. Become a helper at a children's hospital or visit people with disabilities.
29. Offer to help friends whose parents are frail or unwell.
30. Try to remain calm in the face of a loved one's tired and irritable conduct.
31. Offer to take an elderly neighbour's dog for a walk.
32. Write a letter of gratitude and appreciation to your doctor, nurse or teacher.
33. Help locally, or travel further afield, when a natural disaster strikes.
34. Send well-wishes of strength to people who face disappointment, discomfort, or pain.
35. Audit your investments to ensure you support companies that are compassionate.
36. Use your skills in arts or craft to make things for charities to sell and raise money.
37. Spend one holiday a year travelling to poorer parts of the country and offering your help.
38. Chat on the street to a neighbour you know lives alone and rarely gets visitors.
39. Collect a few friends together each year to raise money for an important cause.
40. Speak up when you see wrongdoing.
41. If someone compliments you, try to accept that compliment, and say thank you.
42. If you feel snowed under at work, ask colleagues for help.
43. Try calling a friend when you feel upset or distressed.
44. Ask friends for help if you have a big job to do, such as moving house or cleaning the yard.
45. Identify people you would like a greater connection with and share personal anecdotes.
46. Express your difficult feelings to someone your trust.
47. When someone offers to help, schedule in a time that will work for you both.
48. Explore any fears you have about letting people help you and begin to resolve those fears.
49. Set an intention in the morning that you will practice receiving compassion from others.
50. Identify someone who can be a mentor.

51. Experiment with accepting physical comfort from people who care about you.
52. Practice imagining the way that others hold you fondly in mind.
53. Talk to a friend about the kind of support you would really appreciate from them.
54. When someone you know cares about you asks, 'How are you?' try to answer sincerely.
55. Try recalling experiences where you have felt truly supported by another person.
56. If you unexpectedly can't pay at the shops, graciously accept someone's kind offer to pay.
57. If someone offers you items you really need, accept them and put them to good use.
58. When feeling physical pain, ask others for help, rather than just soldiering on.
59. Remember that allowing someone to help you benefits you and them at the same time.
60. If you feel lost in an unfamiliar place, ask for directions.
61. If someone tells you how much you mean to them, try to let it really sink in.
62. Practice imagery of a compassionate other being there for you during difficult times.
63. Allow someone to hold a door open for you and smile to them as you walk through.
64. Invite caring friends and family into your home for morning tea and a chat.
65. Remember that it does take courage to be open to receiving compassion from others.
66. Practice loving-kindness towards yourself.
67. When a friend calls you and asks how you are, try opening up to them.
68. If someone offers to bring you a meal, graciously accept.
69. Return phone calls from family or friends, even if you are feeling stressed.
70. Stop and practice one minute of soothing rhythm breathing 10 times a day.
71. Find time to read a book or watch a movie.
72. If a health professional recommends homework, see what happens if you follow it through.
73. Go on a retreat, perhaps even a silent retreat.
74. Every day before going to sleep, acknowledge at least one thing you are grateful for that day.

75. Read a book by someone whose good deeds inspire you.
76. Try to appreciate your strengths and qualities.
77. Learn breathing techniques that will help you manage your stress or anxiety.
78. When you feel exhausted, gently bring your body into a compassionate posture.
79. Have a massage.
80. Create a mantra that is compassionate towards yourself and say it every day.
81. When you feel apprehensive, write your anxious self a compassionate letter.
82. Take a long, hot bubble bath.
83. Consider which of your habits are harmful and explore making changes.
84. Cook yourself your favourite meal once in a while.
85. Start doing some light physical exercise.
86. Notice when you put off important tasks in your life and try to complete them instead.
87. Take a self-compassion break in your busy workday.
88. When angry, recognise the vulnerability behind the anger and cultivate safeness.
89. Organise yourself a holiday.
90. Notice the tone of your inner voice and try to make it a warm and friendly tone.
91. Do a regular compassion audit, to reflect on your day and track how you are going.
92. Start a conversation with your critical self, bringing compassion to that part of you.
93. Pause occasionally, and ask yourself, 'What do I need right now?'
94. Find opportunities to express yourself clearly, saying 'no' where that feels right.
95. Find time in the week to be outdoors and in nature.
96. Find time frequently, or even each day, to practice mindfulness meditation.
97. Start to make meal choices that you feel support your overall well-being.
98. Treat yourself with warmth, kindness and compassion when shame arises.
99. Imagine stepping into the role of your Compassionate Self and practice, practice, practice!

Three Pearls

Chapter 11 discussed deepening your compassion, including many very practical ideas and actions. Write your three pearls from Chapter 11 in your *Personal Practice Workbook*.

Chapter 12

Where To From Here?

Pulling it all together...

Life can be difficult. In fact, suffering is a part of life. We cannot avoid it.

And once we are born, we begin to have experiences that we also do not get to choose. We have certain attachment experiences, relational experiences, perhaps trauma, and all of this interacts with our human brains to shape who we become. We could become many possible versions of ourselves, but much of who we become is dictated by our experiences. And it is through all of this that we can sometimes suffer more.

> *This is not your fault, but it is your responsibility.*

But the human brain is at once challenging and incredible. Evolution has provided us with some of the antidote to our suffering: compassion!

> *Compassion is a sensitivity to suffering in self and others, and a motivation and commitment to try to alleviate and prevent it.*

Compassion arises out of the mammalian caring motivation, with a boost from the human soothing-affiliative system, and finally supercharged by new brain feats of social awareness, empathic understanding, and intentional conduct. And so, we can cultivate this compassionate motivation, practice wisdom, strength and courage, and commitment to being helpful, rather than harmful, to ourselves and others. And we can practice the competencies of compassion, such as sensitivity, non-judgment, empathy, sympathy, care for wellbeing and distress tolerance.

Compassion is in us, and we can bring it to the fore.

So, we start to practice our skills. We bring it back to the body, with a compassionate posture, friendly facial expression and voice tone, and soothing rhythm breathing. We use imagery, cultivating feelings of safeness and security through safe place imagery, a sense of our ideal compassionate other, and a sense of our own ideal Compassionate Self.

We begin to explore our multiple selves, becoming acquainted with the Angry Self, Anxious Self, and Sad Self. And we begin a conversation between these multiple selves and our Compassionate Self. The Compassionate Self begins to calm, quiet, and soothe the multiple selves without trying to force them out or getting rid of them.

*The Compassionate Self can bring
our multiple selves into balance.*

We try the Compassionate Self on for size, adopting the character through a kind of method acting approach, walking around in it, experimenting, seeing what it feels like. Gradually, bit by bit, over time, we start to embody the Compassionate Self.

When it feels right, we can bring our Compassionate Self to other aspects of ourselves, especially the critical self, and also the self-conscious emotions of shame, humiliation and guilt. We can use body practices and imagery to allow the sadness, grief, remorse and regret, and soften the anger at the self, as well as the self-blame, self-hate, self-attack and self-disgust.

We can bring the Compassionate Self to our own darkside.

And when the suffering arises out of interpersonal hurt or harm, we practice forgiveness, not condoning the conduct or necessarily reconciling with the person, but forgiving to let go of our anger and rage, and move on from desires of retaliation and vengeance.

And we can practice empathy and reflective listening, developing our communication through compassionate assertiveness, moving from competition to conciliation, expressing our needs and understanding the needs of others. Perhaps we even begin to express appreciation of others, and open ourselves up to others appreciating us.

Compassion is about Prevention

As human beings, we are all expected to continue having ups and downs and challenges. But that's okay, because we're not expecting to always have a smooth run, and this is exactly what the Compassionate Self can help us with. With the Compassionate Self alongside us, we can be ready and equipped to face whatever life might present.

Take up the position of the Compassionate Self, with all its wisdom, strength and courage, and commitment to being helpful, and consider the following three questions. If you like, you can write down your thoughts in your *Personal Practice Workbook*.

- What are the top three things you could do on a regular basis that would involve offering *compassion to others*?
- What are the top three things you could do on a regular basis that would involve opening yourself to receiving *compassion from others*?
- What are the top three things you could do on a regular basis that would involve offering compassion to yourself, or *self-compassion*?

And Compassion is about Alleviating Suffering

Our compassion can include a focus on preventing suffering, but we also have to be ready to work to alleviate suffering when it occurs.

Looking ahead, what are the top ten possible scenarios that might arise in the coming days, weeks or months that will cause you disappointment, discomfort or pain. Take your time here. Space is provided in your *Personal Practice Workbook* to gently work through the possibilities. Such a list is challenging to write, and you may feel your threat system activating. But see what sorts of difficult situations could be ahead for you.

Now, brainstorm the kinds of compassionate behaviours across the three flows in order to respond to these difficult situations and write your thoughts in your *Personal Practice Workbook*.

If you were to face a difficult life situation…

- What would be some examples of behaviours in which you offer *compassion to others*?
- What would be some examples of behaviours in which you might open yourself to *receiving compassion from others*?
- What would be some examples of behaviours in which you might offer *compassion to yourself*?

And Finally, Sending You Compassionate Wishes

Thank you for spending the time and effort to read this book. I do hope it has been clear, engaging and useful. And, more than anything, I hope it has helped you to become well-acquainted with your Compassionate Self!

We have complex brains, and inside these brains of ours are deep wells. It can be a bit mucky down there, and they can cough up some unpleasant stuff. But in these same brains, we also possess all that we need to live a rich, satisfying and deeply fulfilling life. We have a constant wellspring of compassion!

All we need to do is learn to activate our own compassionate response, practice it and eventually embody it, and it will be there for the whole of our lives. Our Compassionate Self is always alongside us, as a guide or mentor, helping us navigate all that it is to be alive. Keep going with it. Keep practising. Such a journey can be so rewarding, and, of course, helps us all to suffer a little less.

And beyond suffering, the Compassionate Self can take us to a place of genuine flourishing.

May you be safe.

May you be peaceful.

May you be healthy.

May you live with ease.

May you be free from suffering.

May you be happy.

May you flourish.

Further Reading

Cooper, M. (2013). *The compassionate mind approach to reducing stress.* London, UK: Robinson.

Fraser, C., & Doyle Fraser, H. (2019). *Freedom: How teens can use mindful compassion to thrive in a chaotic world and grow a purpose-driven life.* Dublin, OH: Calliope House Press.

Gilbert, P. (2009). *The compassionate mind.* London, UK: Constable & Robinson.

Gilbert, P. (2017). *Living like crazy.* York, UK: Annwyn House.

Goss, K. (2011). *The compassionate mind approach to beating overeating: Using compassion focused therapy.* London, UK: Robinson.

Henderson, L. (2010). *Improving social confidence and reducing shyness using compassion focused therapy.* London, UK: Robinson.

Irons, C., & Beaumont, E. (2017). *The compassionate mind workbook: A step-by-step guide to developing your compassionate self.* London, UK: Robinson.

Irons, C. (2019). *The compassionate mind approach to difficult emotions: Using compassion focused therapy.* London, UK: Robinson.

Kolts, R. L. (2012). *The compassionate mind approach to managing your anger: Using compassion focused therapy.* London, UK: Robinson.

Lee, D. (2012). *The compassionate mind approach to recovering from trauma: Using compassion focused therapy.* London, UK: Robinson.

Tirch, D. (2012). *The compassionate mind approach to overcoming anxiety: Using compassion focused therapy.* London, UK: Robinson.

Wellford, M. (2012). *The compassionate mind approach to building your self-confidence: Using compassion focused therapy.* London, UK: Robinson.

Lightning Source UK Ltd.
Milton Keynes UK
UKHW021913010121
376256UK00005B/411